COMMON BIRDS

IN

OMAN

AN IDENTIFICATION GUIDE

2ND EDITION

HANNE & JENS ERIKSEN

Sponsored by

SULTANATE OF
oman
Ministry of Tourism

Muscat Pharmacy & Stores LLC

Al Roya Press & Publishing House

P. O. Box 343, Postal Code 118, Al Harthy Complex, Muscat, Sultanate of Oman
Tel: (968) 24479888, Fax: (968) 24479889
E-mail: alroya@omantel.net.om   www.alroya.net

Al Roya Press & Publishing House

P. O. Box 343, Postal Code 118,
Al Harthy Complex, Muscat,
Sultanate of Oman
Tel: (968) 24479888, Fax: (968) 24479889
E-mail: alroya@omantel.net.om
www.alroya.net

Publisher
Hatim Al Taie

Text & Photographs
© Hanne & Jens Eriksen

Maps
© Hanne & Jens Eriksen

Design and Layout
Jens Eriksen

First edition © 2005

2nd edition © 2010
ISBN 978-9948-15-327-6

Acknowledgements
The authors wish to thank the many birdwatchers who, over the years, have sent in their sightings and thereby have given us a much clearer picture of which birds are found where and at what time of the year. We also thank members of the Oman Bird Records Committee, past and present, for their contributions to establishing a reliable list of the birds of Oman. Finally, we thank the Ministry of Tourism, Muscat Pharmacy and Haya Water for their generous sponsorship of this book.

August 2010
Hanne & Jens Eriksen

Stonechat

Printed by:
Al Anan Printing Press, Muscat

Greater Flamingo

Table of Contents

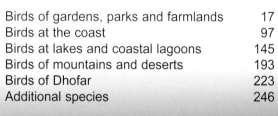

African Silverbill

Greater Flamingo

Introduction

Why watch birds? There are probably as many answers to this question as there are birdwatchers. But the reasons given have many things in common. Birds are by far the most conspicuous group of animals. They can be studied any time of day (or night), any time of the year and any place on earth. The birdwatcher can be as young as five, as old as 105 or anything in between. Birds are lively, colourful, have beautiful songs, build intricate nests to raise their families, and migrate huge distances between continents.

Birdwatching can be done alone or as a social event with friends. It can be done on a casual basis learning only the names of birds seen on a day at the beach. Or, a good birdwatching area may be visited to seek out special birds. It may be a lifelong passion with travels to far flung places on earth to find many wonderful and exotic species. Birdwatchers may keep a list of birds seen in their gardens or in their country, a list of birds seen in a given year, or a lifelist. It is no wonder, then, that birdwatching is one of the fastest growing hobbies in many parts of the world.

Identifying birds can be an enormous challenge. With some 10,000 species of birds in the world - and 498 species recognized in Oman - it would be a daunting task to learn them all. As male and female birds, young and old, and summer and winter may all bring different plumages, the complexity involved in bird identification quickly becomes apparent. Nobody has seen all the birds in the world. The world record is about 8,600 species seen by a single person. Our good friend and co-author of other books on birds in Oman, Dave Sargeant, has topped the 7,800 mark.

But birdwatching is first and foremost an enjoyable hobby. To be able to add a name to that flying creature over the coast or in the garden instantly makes it more interesting. We hope with this field guide to be able to help you get started and add another dimension to your outings in Oman.

Three generations looking for birds near Muscat

About this book

At present, 498 species of birds have been seen in Oman. This is an impressive number considering that a large proportion of the country is desert and that there are no real forests. For the new birdwatcher, that many species with all the variations in appearance of each species due to sex, age, and time of year, can make it quite difficult to be confident about an identification. However, of the 498 species, about 150 are vagrants having been seen less than 10 times. Many others are considered rare and are also unlikely to be encountered. In this guide we have included all species considered abundant or common as well as many species that are fairly common and that are quite easy to identify - 250 species in all. So the task is greatly reduced. In the beginning, concentrate on the common and conspicuous species and gradually, you will improve your identification skills. Later you may want to tackle the more difficult ones, the 'LBJs' ('little brown jobs'). You will undoubtedly come across a bird that just doesn't seem to be in the book. Don't worry. Even experts will sometimes have to let a bird pass unidentified. To simplify the task of identification further, we have grouped the species together according to habitat. This has many advantages, but may also lead to pitfalls. If you are in a park or garden in north Oman, you should see species like the White-spectacled Bulbul, Laughing Dove, Purple Sunbird, Graceful Prinia, Indian Roller and Common Myna among others. Forget about these species if you are at the coast. In Salalah, you will not see Purple Sunbirds, Indian Rollers and Common Mynas. Great Cormorants may well be seen at Al Ansab Lagoons, but its 'cousin', the Socotra Cormorant occurs only at sea. Thus, identifying the habitat cuts down the number of different species to be expected. The trouble is, however, that some birds - like the Laughing Dove - are widespread and may be

Indian Roller

encountered in more than one habitat. Still, when trying to identify a new bird, start looking in the habitat section that fits best.

We have identified four different habitats and added a section on Dhofar. The reason for the latter is that there are a number of very common birds in the Salalah area that are never seen north of the Dhofar mountains. Within each habitat the most common birds are presented first. Each habitat has been colour coded at the upper left or right hand corner of the page for easy reference and they are:

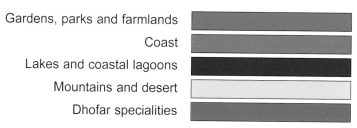

Gardens, parks and farmlands

Coast

Lakes and coastal lagoons

Mountains and desert

Dhofar specialities

Distribution of birds. When we say a species is common this is only true in the right habitat and at the right time of the year. The spectacular Red-billed Tropicbirds are common, but only along coastal cliffs and only during the breeding season from April to October. The rest of the year they stay far out at sea and can be very difficult to find. For the distribution maps the following colour coding has been used:

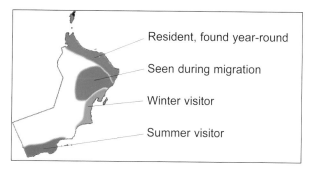

Resident, found year-round

Seen during migration

Winter visitor

Summer visitor

For seasonal changes the following coding has been used:

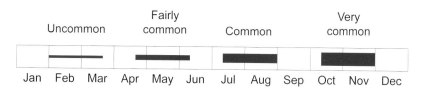

Uncommon   Fairly common   Common   Very common

Jan Feb Mar Apr May Jun Jul Aug Sep Oct Nov Dec

How to watch birds

To get started in birdwatching you need four 'things': a pair of binoculars, a notebook, a basic field guide (like this one), and curiosity about the natural world. Thus, it does not have to be an expensive hobby. Sure, you can spend a small fortune by adding a telescope, expensive cameras and telephoto lenses and you could travel all over the world in search of new species. However, you can gain much satisfaction and enjoyment by simply opening your eyes and ears and birdwatch in your own neighbourhood.

To fully appreciate birds, you have to see some plumage details and for this a good pair of binoculars is essential. A notebook is useful for making a list of what you see in a particular area. Later when visiting the same area a comparison can be made and you will soon begin to appreciate that some birds may be seen during almost every visit, while others are only seen at a certain time of the year. If you see a bird you cannot identify, try to make a drawing of it no matter how poor. When you come home you can study the field guide in more detail or perhaps a month or a year later when you have more experience, you may be able to identify the bird from the drawing.

With so many birds around us, getting started in birdwatching may seem bewildering. Try, however, to get familiar with the most common birds first. When you know these, you can expand by making comparisons with the familiar ones: 'the new bird was slightly smaller than a White-spectacled Bulbul, but bigger than a House Sparrow.' This already narrows down the number of possibilities.

Binoculars

The only major purchase needed to start birdwatching is a good pair of binoculars. You should expect to pay about RO 40-50 for a decent pair. Cheaper ones are available and may seem adequate at first, but they are probably not dustproof and within a short time in the field they may be filled with dust and sand. You could spend a lot more, RO 500 or more, but this is not really necessary when starting out.

What to look for when buying? Binoculars are rated with two numbers, such as 7 x 35, 8 x 40, 10 x 42 or something similar. The first number is the magnification. You might think the more the better, but magnification greater than ten times is difficult to hold steady enough for good viewing. The second number is the diameter, in mm, of the big lens in front, the objective lens. The bigger the lens, the brighter the view through the binoculars. In Oman, however, the light is usually so bright you will not need an objective lens bigger than 40 mm. Also remember, that the bigger the magnification and the bigger the lenses, the heavier the binoculars. This is important as you may need to carry them around your neck for several hours at a time. All in all, the ideal combination of magnification and objective size will be something similar to the numbers mentioned above.

When buying, make sure you test the binoculars yourself, preferably outside the store. Do they feel comfortable in the hand and around your neck? Is the focusing wheel easy to reach and operate with your fingers? Is the view through the binuculars clear and sharp all the way to the edges? Are the colours true to life? Some binoculars have yellow coating on the objectives. This may be fine if you want to watch boat races, but pretty useless for birdwatching. If you wear glasses, make sure the eye cups on the binoculars can be folded down so you can get a full view without having to remove your glasses each time.

RO 500   RO 50

How to identify birds

Successful bird identification requires a fair bit of skill from the observer. The bird's plumage and colours are obviously important clues, but there are many more. When you come across a new species try to work through its features in a systematic way. What is its size in relation to birds you already know? Are there any obvious features like a wing bar, a conspicuous eye ring, or brightly coloured feather tracts? What is the size, shape and colour of its bill? Of its legs? With experience the call and song of birds can also help with identification.

As with any new subject there are a few terms that are useful to know in describing a bird. Without going into too much detail, some important ones are illustrated below.

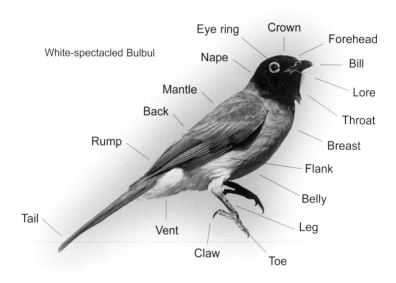

White-spectacled Bulbul

Eye ring · Crown · Forehead · Nape · Bill · Mantle · Lore · Back · Throat · Rump · Breast · Flank · Belly · Tail · Vent · Leg · Claw · Toe

Ear coverts · Wing bars · Citrine Wagtail

Upper mandible · Supercilium · Eye stripe · Lower mandible · Cinnamon-breasted Bunting

Wings and tail. In flight, the shape of the wings and tail can give important clues to the identification of a new bird. The Egyptian Vulture is black and white as an adult and is easy to identify, but younger birds can be all dark or mottled black and white. In all ages, though, the Egyptian Vulture has a wedge-shaped tail which is an excellent identification feature. Eagles have large wings and rounded tails. If seen well you can count seven 'fingers,' the primaries that make up the tip of the wing. The two large white-headed gulls - Caspian Gull and Heuglin's Gull - that are so common along the beaches in winter can be difficult to tell apart. The black in the wingtip of the Caspian Gull is less extensive and the line between black and white more abrupt than in the Heuglin's Gull.

The young (*juvenile*) Egyptian Vulture is all mottled dark, but can be identified on the shape of its tail

An adult Egyptian Vulture is easy to identify on its creamy white and black plumage and the wedge-shaped tail

Steppe Eagle

Seven 'fingers' show this is an eagle

Secondaries

Primaries, 10 in all

Caspian Gull

Heuglin's Gull

Less black in wingtip

Black in wingtip more extensive

Bills. Birds' bills come in all shapes and sizes and give a good indication of the food the birds consume and their feeding habits. An eagle has a sharp and powerful bill for tearing meat apart. Sparrows and finches have short, stubby bills indicating they are mainly seed eaters, while warblers, pipits and wagtails have fine, pointed bills well suited for eating insects. Waders tend to have long bills for seeking food in the mud, but several species of waders can feed side by side as they differ in bill length and therefore find food at different depths, hence they do not compete with one another. Spoonbills and flamingos have specialized bills and specialized feeding techniques. The Eurasian Spoonbill walks in shallow water, moving the slightly open bill from side to side, grabbing small food items that wash into its bill. Flamingos and some ducks have lamellae not unlike baleen whales. They sieve the water for small organisms by pumping water through the lamellae. Look carefully at the bill next time you see a bird - it is an important identification feature.

Steppe Eagle
a meat eater

Eurasian Spoonbill
a specialized feeder

Greater Flamingo
a specialized feeder

Eurasian Curlew
seeking food on mudflats

African Silverbill
a seed eater

Citrine Wagtail
an insect eater

Common Redshank
seeking food on mudflats

Legs and feet. The legs of birds are another identification characteristic. Long legs like those of herons, storks, spoonbills and flamingos suggest the bird seeks its food by wading in quite deep water. The powerful legs and claws of the Osprey are useful for catching and holding on to slippery fish - its only diet. Passerines or perching birds (bulbuls, sparrows etc.) have feet that hold on to a branch even while the bird is asleep. If you see a small passerine on the ground, look carefully how the bird moves. Does it hop like a sparrow or does it walk like a starling? Terns have small, feeble feet and can barely walk on the beach. Ducks have webbed feet and are excellent swimmers.

Whiskered Tern

Greater Flamingo

Long legs, wading in deep water

Small legs, no good for catching fish

Grey Francolin

Indian Silverbill

Powerful legs, for running

Passerine or perching bird

Osprey

Mallard

Webbed feet, for swimming

Powerful legs, for catching fish

Where to watch birds in Oman

Although birds can be found almost anywhere in the country, they are not uniformly distributed. To see birds beyond the most common ones

you will have to visit several different places at the right time of the year. Below we list a few of the many good sites in Oman. For more details and how to find each site, we recommend getting our *Birdwatching guide to Oman, second edition*, available at leading bookshops. This guide lists over 60 of the best sites in Oman with a map of each site and which birds can be expected. It also gives other useful information for the birdwatcher, such as road conditions along with car rental and hotel contact details throughout the country.

Muscat area. One of the best places to start birdwatching and to get to know the most common and familiar birds is Al Qurm Natural Park. Year-round you can find three species of bulbuls, Graceful Prinia, Laughing Dove, Green Bee-eater and Purple Sunbird to name but a few. The coastal area may hold a variety of herons, waders, gulls and terns. Al Ansab Lagoons is another excellent area and a good place for various eagles and waterbirds.

Al Batinah coast. Ras As Sawadi is good for waders, gulls, terns and, in summer, Sooty Falcon. The farmlands near Sohar are a favourite place for larks, pipits, wagtails and numerous other species, especially during migration. The mangroves at Liwa and Shinas are home to the localized Collared Kingfisher.

White Wagtail

Musandam. The many birds found here during winter and spring makes Musandam well worth a visit. Socotra Cormorants are often found along the coast near Khasab.

Ash Sharqiyyah region. The beaches near Ras Al Hadd will have gulls and terns and are good places for observing bird migration. With luck the spectacular Red-billed Tropicbird may put in an appearance. At Khawr Jirama Crab-plovers may be seen among other waders.

Al Hajar mountains. A visit to the northern mountains will not produce a big bird list, but interesting species like the huge Lappet-faced Vulture may be seen soaring above.

Masirah and Barr Al Hikman. Though more difficult to reach, these areas will produce huge numbers of birds, in particular herons, waders, gulls and terns. Masirah has proven to be a great place for rare and unusual birds, especially during migration.

Central desert. A drive from Muscat to Salalah will not produce many birds, but a stop at the various resthouses and at Muntasar may be rewarded with excellent sightings. With its lush gardens the motels at Al Ghaftayn and Qatbit are particularly good for birdwatching as many birds make a stopover here during migration. The permanent water at Muntasar attracts sandgrouse by the hundreds.

Dhofar. A visit to Salalah is a must for the serious birdwatcher as the Dhofar region has a long list of birds not found elsewhere in Oman. The many coastal lagoons will hold Greater Flamingos, Eurasian Spoonbills and Glossy Ibises throughout the year, and a variety of ducks during winter. The gardens and foothills at Ayn Razat and Ayn Hamran are good places for the Dhofar specialities, such as Abyssinian White-eye, Cinnamon-breasted Bunting, African Paradise Flycatcher, Rüppell's Weaver, Shining and Palestine Sunbirds, Blackstarts and many other common birds. Seabirds can be observed from Mirbat.

Glossy Ibises at sunset

Birdwatching code of conduct

While birdwatching, it is worth to remember that we are here to enjoy the birds. In our eagerness to get closer to the birds to obtain better views we should not forget that the welfare of the birds is top priority. Please adhere to this simple 'birdwatching code of conduct:'

Never harass the birds unduly. This is especially true if you are near a nest. Do not alter anything around the nest which might invite a predator when you leave.

If birdwatching on private land, make sure to ask permission first. Landowners are normally happy to have visiting birdwatchers, but simple courtesy requires we ask first.

When birdwatching with a group make sure to move quietly and slowly so as not to disturb the birds and ruin other birdwatchers' chances to see them.

When out for a picnic or camping trip, please bring all rubbish back with you.

Remember, it is forbidden in Oman by law to trap, shoot, kill and harass birds and other living creatures.

More information

If you are looking for more information on birds and birdwatching in Oman, check out our website www.BirdsOman.com. It is updated regularly and gives information on the latest sightings of unusual birds. Please also send in your own bird records to the Oman Bird Records Committee, which keeps a database of all bird observations in Oman. Instructions on how to submit your records can be found on the above website.

A more comprehensive field guide for the region is *Birds of the Middle East* by Richard Porter and Simon Aspinall (Helm Field Guides, 2010).

The *Oman Bird List, Edition 6* by J. Eriksen, R. Victor and D. E. Sargeant (2003) gives the status and distribution of all the bird species accepted in the Sultanate of Oman.

The *Birdwatching guide to Oman, second edition* by D. E. Sargeant and H. & J. Eriksen (2008) and the Arabic translation in 2002 of the first edition list all the best birdwatching sites in Oman, how to find them and what to expect when you get there.

Birds of gardens, parks and farmlands

This is where birdwatching starts. If you have access to a large garden with trees and lawns you should have plenty of birds around you. Alternatively, visit any of the parks in the Capital area - such as Al Qurm Park - and birds will be plentiful. Here are a few of the common birds seen in this habitat.

Cattle Egret

White-spectacled Bulbul

Graceful Prinia

Green Bee-eater

Laughing Dove

Purple Sunbird

Grey Francolin

Bulbuls are typical garden birds and they are noisy, conspicuous and found in their range wherever there are trees and bushes.

White-spectacled Bulbul *Pycnonotus xanthopygos*
20 cm

The White-spectacled Bulbul is one of our most common and familiar birds. It is like an alarm clock - its delightful song is the first to be heard in the morning. Several birds and family groups visit fruiting trees and the fleshy berries of the Christ-thorn tree are a favourite food. May sometimes be confused with the Red-vented Bulbul if the vent (undertail feathers) is not seen well. However, that species has a white rump and dark eyes.

| Jan | Feb | Mar | Apr | May | Jun | Jul | Aug | Sep | Oct | Nov | Dec |

The two species below have been introduced in the Muscat area and are now spreading. Expected to become more common in the future.

White-eared Bulbul

Pycnonotus leucotis
20 cm

Not nearly as common as the White-spectacled Bulbul, but rapidly spreading and now regularly found in hotel gardens in Muscat and Al Qurm Natural Park. Now also common in Sohar and in the mangroves at Liwa and Shinas suggesting further expansions can be expected.

Red-vented Bulbul

Pycnonotus cafer
20 cm

This is the least common of the three bulbuls, but it is easy to find in the gardens at Ras As Sawadi Beach Resort in north Oman. Other likely places are Al Qurm Natural Park, hotel gardens around Muscat and at Sultan Qaboos University.

These two birds are the smallest birds found in Oman, but they are among the noisiest.

Graceful Prinia

Prinia gracilis
10 cm

Abundant resident bird in both north and south Oman. Found wherever there are trees and bushes in gardens and parks. Also plentiful in reedbeds around lakes and lagoons such as Al Ansab Lagoons near Muscat and the khawrs near Salalah.

You will probably hear the Graceful Prinia before you see it. It hides in dense vegetation much of the time except when it sings from a perch right out in the open. The song is a loud, monotonous and continuous 'zeee-tit zeee-tit zeee-tit.' Usually quite tame and very active with its long tail swaying from side to side or up and down. The male and female look alike. The nest is like a ball of grass with an entrance hole on the side.

Jan Feb Mar Apr May Jun Jul Aug Sep Oct Nov Dec

Purple Sunbird

Cinnyris asiaticus
10 cm

Female

Male, breeding
January - June

Male, non-breeding
July - December

Abundant resident, but only in northern Oman and Musandam. Found wherever there are trees and bushes in gardens and parks. Will come to a hummingbird feeder with red-coloured sugar water, though sunbirds are not related to hummingbirds.

This delightful little bird is very easy to see on account of its noisy and conspicuous nature. The male in the breeding season is constantly chasing other males out of his territory. Outside the breeding season - from August to December - the male loses his purple gloss and is yellowish below with a black line down the front. The female is more dull looking. She builds an elaborate, oblong nest hanging from a branch often close to a house.

| Jan | Feb | Mar | Apr | May | Jun | Jul | Aug | Sep | Oct | Nov | Dec |

The two rollers commonly found in Oman look somewhat alike, but they have different distributions. The European Roller is found only during migration, but could turn up anywhere then. The Indian Roller is resident, but found only in north Oman.

European Roller

Coracias garrulus
30 cm

Spring

Autumn

A passage migrant that is common only during a short time in late April and early May. Less common during the autumn passage. At these times the European Roller can turn up just about anywhere - in parks and wadis, sometimes even in the middle of the desert.

In spring the European Roller is a brilliant bird with its turquoise-blue head and wings and the reddish-brown back. In autumn it can look very worn and quite pale. Easy to tell from the Indian Roller by its blue head. A roller found outside north Oman is likely to be a European Roller. The favourite food is beetles and grasshoppers. The bird may sit motionless in a tree for a long time, then swoop down to seize its prey on the ground.

| Jan | Feb | Mar | Apr | May | Jun | Jul | Aug | Sep | Oct | Nov | Dec |

Indian Roller

Coracias benghalensis
30 cm

Abundant resident, but found only in north Oman and Musandam. Particularly common at Al Qurm Natural Park near Muscat, along the main highway from Muscat to the border with UAE and on farmlands. In autumn up to 500 birds have been seen at Sun Farms near Sohar.

Sitting quietly waiting for prey to turn up, the Indian Roller is not very conspicuous, but in flight the brilliant blue wings and tail give the bird away instantly. Rollers are named for their territorial displays in spring when the birds can be seen rolling in the air. An intruder into the territory will be chased away with fierce aerial pursuits and loud raucous noises. The birds even make mock attacks on people who come too close.

Jan   Feb   Mar   Apr   May   Jun   Jul   Aug   Sep   Oct   Nov   Dec

Two common birds with a shared diet. The shape of their bill shows that they are mainly seed eaters.

House Sparrow

Passer domesticus
15 cm

Male

Female

House Sparrows are familiar birds in towns and villages in northern Oman. Lately they have spread and small colonies are now found at Al Ghabah and Al Ghaftayn resthouses in the central desert, near Hayma and at Thumrayt.

Usually, House Sparrows are associated with human habitation and the birds often use buildings for their nest sites. At dusk hundreds of birds may gather in a single tree with much chirping to settle in for the night. Sparrows are part of the weaver family and when nesting they sometimes build large complexes with many apartments. House Sparrows spend much time on the ground and often engage in dust bathing.

| Jan | Feb | Mar | Apr | May | Jun | Jul | Aug | Sep | Oct | Nov | Dec |

24

Indian Silverbill

Lonchura malabarica
11 cm

Indian Silverbills are most common on farmlands and waste areas where there is a good supply of grass seed. Good places to look for them are at Qurayyat and the farms near Sohar, but they are common over much of Al Batinah.

These small birds move around in flocks looking for food: grass with ripe seeds. They sit on the grass stems while feeding or they hold down a stem with one foot while they strip the grass of seeds. They make a high-pitched tinkling call and soon the flock takes off in search of another good food supply. In south Oman the Indian Silverbill is replaced by the African Silverbill with a dark rump. Silverbills are sometimes kept as cage birds.

Jan   Feb   Mar   Apr   May   Jun   Jul   Aug   Sep   Oct   Nov   Dec

Two species alien to Oman and originating in India. The Common Myna is a recent addition from a few escaped cage birds about 25 years ago. Since then they have spread explosively over the whole of Al Batinah and further expansions can be expected.

Common Myna

Acridotheres tristis
24 cm

Now abundant over most of Al Batinah coast and seen in large flocks throughout the year. Particularly common in hotel gardens, at Al Qurm Natural Park and at farmlands near Sohar where up to 3,000 birds have been seen together. Increasingly common in Salalah as well.

The Common Myna is a member of the starling family. It is big, bold and aggressive and will chase other birds away from food supplies and nesting sites. Like other starlings it walks rather than hops when on the ground. In flight the large, white wing patches are conspicuous. Always seen in noisy flocks. The Common Myna is not a welcome guest as it competes with native birds. It will be interesting to see if it spreads further.

| Jan | Feb | Mar | Apr | May | Jun | Jul | Aug | Sep | Oct | Nov | Dec |

Rose-ringed Parakeet

Psittacula krameri
40 cm

Female

Male

Common resident over much of Al Batinah and Musandam and lately also in the Salalah area. In Muscat, hundreds of birds come to roost each evening at the Intercontinental Hotel and Crowne Plaza Hotel gardens and the noise when so many birds gather can be deafening.

Despite its colourful plumage the Rose-ringed Parakeet (previously called the Ring-necked Parakeet) can be difficult to see in the tree tops. Most often it is heard before it is seen and in flight the long tail is unmistakable. Only the male has the pink and black neck band. Rose-ringed Parakeets are sociable birds that move around in flocks of variable sizes looking for food. Large numbers sometimes descend on corn fields.

| Jan | Feb | Mar | Apr | May | Jun | Jul | Aug | Sep | Oct | Nov | Dec |

Our two most common doves can be seen over most of the country avoiding only the most inhospitable areas of the Empty Quarter.

Laughing Dove

Streptopelia senegalensis
25 cm

The Laughing Dove is one of the most common and widespread birds in Oman. It is found throughout the year in parks and gardens, towns and villages, wadis and mountains and often associated with human habitation.

The Laughing Dove is named after its song that sounds like a laughter. This delightful little dove is seen everywhere in trees or on the ground, even on parking lots and quiet roads and will turn up wherever there is a bit of food. Rather tame and confiding. The nest is a flimsy structure of twigs in a tree and as with all doves, two white eggs are laid. Male and female look alike, but young birds lack the black spots on the side of the neck.

Jan	Feb	Mar	Apr	May	Jun	Jul	Aug	Sep	Oct	Nov	Dec

Eurasian Collared Dove

Streptopelia decaocto
28 cm

The Eurasian Collared Dove is a common resident in north and south Oman and an abundant passage migrant and winter visitor thoughout most of the country. Particularly numerous on farmlands near Sohar and Salalah where flocks of several thousands may be seen.

The Eurasian Collared Dove is somewhat larger than the Laughing Dove. It is a shy bird and does not seek human company. Sexes are alike and the black collar on the neck makes it easy to identify. The song is a monotonous, three-syllable 'to-HOO-ho' with emphasis on the second syllable and repeated endlessly. Most often seen in large flocks feeding on the ground on farms and wastelands. Also found in mangroves in north Oman.

| Jan | Feb | Mar | Apr | May | Jun | Jul | Aug | Sep | Oct | Nov | Dec |

These two doves are much less common than the two previous ones, but look for them on farmlands in both north and south Oman.

European Turtle Dove

Streptopelia turtur
27 cm

Fairly common to common passage migrant with a few staying to breed over summer. The passage is rather concentrated over a few weeks in spring and autumn. This dove is often found in the company of other doves on farmlands.

The European Turtle Dove is easy to recognise on its black and white neck patch and rufous wings. The song of this bird is a drawn-out, enticing 'turrrrrrrrr,' that is easy to separate from the previous two species. Like other doves it feeds on the ground and flies off if danger approaches. It often perches on electrical wires with other doves. A careful check through all the birds in a flock of doves may reveal a few European Turtle Doves.

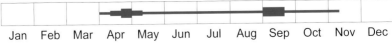

| Jan | Feb | Mar | Apr | May | Jun | Jul | Aug | Sep | Oct | Nov | Dec |

Namaqua Dove

Oena capensis
28 cm

Female

Male

Fairly common breeding resident on farms near Salalah and, increasingly, elsewhere in Oman such as at Sun Farms in Sohar and Al Balid Farm in the desert in Dhofar interior. It is normally encountered in pairs or a few birds together, but large flocks have not been seen in Oman.

A charming little dove that is becoming more and more common. Though its overall size suggests it is at least as big as a European Turtle Dove, half the length of a Namaqua Dove is its extraordinarily long and thin tail; thus, its body size is very small indeed. Often found on the ground where a pair may be seen walking around quietly in search of seeds. The male is unmistakable while the female is more subdued in colour.

	Jan	Feb	Mar	Apr	May	Jun	Jul	Aug	Sep	Oct	Nov	Dec

The two green bee-eaters along with the European Bee-eater (p 34) are among the most colourful birds in Oman.

Green Bee-eater

Merops orientalis
25 cm

Very common breeding resident found both in north and south Oman, though most commonly in the north. It seems to avoid the central desert and Masirah. Particularly common at Al Qurm Natural Park and on farmlands along the Batinah coast.

This well-known and easily recognisable bird is with us year-round. It sits quietly on a branch scanning the surroundings for flying insects. If one is spotted, the bird dashes out, seizes the prey in the bill and returns to the same branch. It may kill the insect by banging it against the branch. Rarely does it come to the ground and when it does, it is most often to have a dust bath. The nest is at the end of a tunnel dug into a bank.

| Jan | Feb | Mar | Apr | May | Jun | Jul | Aug | Sep | Oct | Nov | Dec |

Blue-cheeked Bee-eater

Merops persicus
30 cm

During migration, Blue-cheeked Bee-eaters may turn up anywhere in Oman, but they breed in colonies only along the northern Batinah coast. Though most common on farmlands, it may also be seen coming in to roost in mangroves and reedbeds during migration.

The Blue-cheeked Bee-eater is considerably bigger than the Green Bee-eater and can easily be separated from that species by its yellow and orange throat. Like all bee-eaters the food consists of flying insects, all caught on the wing. These birds nest in large colonies and dig tunnels into a sandy bank or into flat ground. At the end of the tunnel is the nest chamber where eggs and young are well protected.

| Jan | Feb | Mar | Apr | May | Jun | Jul | Aug | Sep | Oct | Nov | Dec |

The third species of bee-eaters regularly found in Oman is the most colourful of all - just about every colour of the rainbow is represented.

European Bee-eater

Merops apiaster
28 cm

The European Bee-eater is still quite common during migration, but has declined dramatically in recent years. It used to nest regularly on the northern Batinah coast and still does so in some areas. Look for it on electrical wires along the highway between Khaburah and Sohar.

It is a jewel of a bird that arrives in late March or early April having spent the winter in Africa. Like other bee-eaters, it may be seen flying over grassy fields in search of flying insects: grasshoppers, butterflies, dragonflies and flying ants. In flight it resembles the Blue-cheeked Bee-eater (p 33), but when seen well it is unmistakable. The nest is at the end of a long tunnel dug into a sandy bank or into the side of a field well.

| Jan | Feb | Mar | Apr | May | Jun | Jul | Aug | Sep | Oct | Nov | Dec |

The Eurasian Hoopoe or 'hod-hod' in Arabic is unique with its impressive crest. It is named for its call that can be heard during spring.

Eurasian Hoopoe

Upupa epops
28 cm

The Eurasian Hoopoe is a common passage migrant and winter visitor. A few birds stay to breed in woodlands along the northern Batinah coast. Look for this bird on farmlands near Sohar and in parks near Salalah such as Ayn Hamran.

This well-known bird is quite unmistakable. Normally the crest lies flat over the head and is raised only when the bird gets excited. It spends much time on the ground digging for larvae with its long decurved bill. When disturbed the bird flies up for a short distance and lands raising its crest. In flight the black and white wing pattern is conspicuous. The nest is in a hole in a tree or in a crevice between rocks.

Jan	Feb	Mar	Apr	May	Jun	Jul	Aug	Sep	Oct	Nov	Dec

These two species belong to the partridge family, but they vary greatly in size and ease of finding. The Grey Francolin is common year-round in the Muscat area while the Common Quail is seen mostly on migration.

Grey Francolin

Francolinus pondicerianus
30 cm

Grey Francolins are very common all over the capital area and on farmlands on Al Batinah. Look for them in Al Qurm Natural Park and on the lawns along the main highway. They have taken to these newly created habitats and simply ignore the cars zooming by.

Grey Francolins are often heard before they are seen. They make a tremendous chattering noise in the mornings and evenings - one bird starts up and all others in the area join in for a big chorus. The birds spend most of their time on the ground looking for seeds. With their strong bill and feet they scrape away the surface to reveal food below. Even when only half grown the chicks are able to fly.

| Jan | Feb | Mar | Apr | May | Jun | Jul | Aug | Sep | Oct | Nov | Dec |

Common Quail

Coturnix coturnix
18 cm

A small bird that can be very difficult to spot as it normally hides in long grass. Look for it in the early morning and late afternoon at Al Qurm Natural Park and Sun Farms near Sohar. Even here it is difficult to get a good view - the bird will run away and quickly seek shelter.

The Common Quail is never seen in big numbers. You normally come across just a single bird and most often just by accident. Because of its secretive habits, the Common Quail is probably more common than we think as, surely, many birds pass through the country unnoticed. When seen well it is not difficult to identify. It simply looks like a very small, stripy chicken. Male and female differ slightly with the male having heavier streaking on the face.

| Jan | Feb | Mar | Apr | May | Jun | Jul | Aug | Sep | Oct | Nov | Dec |

These two larks are rather dull brownish-grey in colour. Both have crests, though that of the Crested Lark is the most impressive.

Crested Lark

Galerida cristata
17 cm

This common lark can be found in just about any habitat, but it is most common in wide open areas such as farmlands and in the desert. Difficult to miss on farms on the Batinah and around Salalah, but open areas in Al Qurm Natural Park are good places to look for it, too.

The Crested Lark is our most common and conspicuous lark. The crest is always raised and the tip is pointed. Through much of the year the Crested Lark can be heard and the song is very pleasing, delivered either from a low bush or in flight. Male and female look the same and the pair is often seen together on the ground looking for food, mainly insects. The nest is on the ground under a bush or tuft of grass.

| Jan | Feb | Mar | Apr | May | Jun | Jul | Aug | Sep | Oct | Nov | Dec |

Eurasian Skylark

Alauda arvensis
16 cm

A species much less common than the previous one and more difficult to find and identify. Look for it in grassy fields on farmlands such as those near Sohar and Salalah. Occasionally, a few birds are reported in Al Qurm Natural Park.

Although the Eurasian Skylark can raise its crest when excited, most often the crown feathers lie flat over the head. Good identification features are stripes on the breast and a darkish patch on the cheek. In flight a white trailing edge to the wings and white sides to the tail are visible. While in Oman, Eurasian Skylarks do not sing, but when taking off a call note is heard, like 'chrrriup' that can be a good identification clue once learned.

| Jan | Feb | Mar | Apr | May | Jun | Jul | Aug | Sep | Oct | Nov | Dec |

These two larks are fairly common on farmlands, though the Short-toed Lark can also be found in desert habitat throughout the country.

Greater Short-toed Lark   *Calandrella brachydactyla*

14 cm

The Greater Short-toed Lark is a common passage migrant and winter visitor. Look for it on farmlands around Sohar and Salalah and inland farms such as Al Balid Farm in Dhofar and Mabr Farm near Hayma. A few birds stay to breed in May and June at Sun Farms, Sohar.

The Greater Short-toed Lark, though superficially similar to a Eurasian Skylark, has a reddish crown and lacks the striping on the breast. An excellent identification clue is a black mark on either side of the neck. During winter it is often found in large flocks. When breeding the male sings continuously for several minutes while circling over his territory. The name of this bird is rather misleading as, in fact, it does not have short toes.

| Jan | Feb | Mar | Apr | May | Jun | Jul | Aug | Sep | Oct | Nov | Dec |

Bimaculated Lark

Melanocorypha bimaculata
16 cm

The Bimaculated Lark is a fairly common winter visitor to farmlands in both north and south Oman and occasionally elsewhere. Most observations have come from Sun Farms in Sohar where sizeable flocks are regularly encountered.

Bimaculated Larks can be recognized on the two dark spots on the side of the neck (much bolder than on Greater Short-toed Larks) and the strong, white supercilium that gives the birds an aggressive look. They gather on abandoned fields, especially corn fields, and pick up what kernels they can find. In late winter the birds are rather noisy and a distant flock can sound like a flock of Common Starlings.

Jan Feb Mar Apr May Jun Jul Aug Sep Oct Nov Dec

Unlike the other larks found in Oman, the male and female Black-crowned Sparrow-Larks look very different.

Black-crowned Sparrow-Lark *Eremopterix nigriceps*
12 cm

Male

Female

A striking small bird that can be found in arid country throughout Oman. It is most common, however, on farmlands, but look for it also at the resthouses along the Muscat - Salalah road. In winter, large flocks wander around and can turn up anywhere.

The male Black-crowned Sparrow-Lark is unmistakable with its black and white markings on the head and black underparts. The female is quite different and looks much like other lark species, but can be identified by its small size and thick bill. Normally, of course, males and females are seen together, including outside the breeding season, so identification is rarely a problem. The song is a pleasing, drawn-out whistle of 2-4 notes.

| Jan | Feb | Mar | Apr | May | Jun | Jul | Aug | Sep | Oct | Nov | Dec |

Martins and swallows form a group of birds that spend many daylight hours on the wing in search of food.

Pale Crag Martin

Ptyonoprogne obsoleta
12 cm

Pale Crag Martins are very common resident birds and often associated with human habitation. They can also be found in mountainous areas. Look for them in towns and villages, in Al Qurm Natural Park and the foothill parks near Salalah.

Formerly called African Rock Martin this species is originally a bird of the mountains, but it has taken a liking to our concrete structures and now commonly nests in buildings. The nest is made of mud brought to the nest site in the bird's bill and placed right under the ceiling. Pale Crag Martins lack the dark breast band of Sand Martins (p 44). When seen well in flight the white spots on the undertail are good identification features.

| Jan | Feb | Mar | Apr | May | Jun | Jul | Aug | Sep | Oct | Nov | Dec |

Martins belong to the swallow family, but unlike the Barn and Red-rumped Swallows (p 46-47) they lack the long tail streamers.

Sand Martin

Riparia riparia
12 cm

The Sand Martin is a common passage migrant and winter visitor. It is particularly common during the autumn. Look for it in mixed groups of swallows on farmlands and over lagoons. Good places are farms near Sohar and Salalah, Al Ansab Lagoons and Al Qurm Natural Park.

Though rather dull looking compared with Barn and Red-rumped Swallows, Sand Martins can be identified by the dark breast band. To see the band may require some patience when the birds are flying rapidly over the fields constantly changing direction. If resting on a wire the task of identification is easier. Normally encountered in medium to large flocks, sometimes numbering hundreds of birds.

| Jan | Feb | Mar | Apr | May | Jun | Jul | Aug | Sep | Oct | Nov | Dec |

Common House Martin

Delichon urbicum
13 cm

The Common House Martin is a fairly common passage migrant with a few observations in summer and winter as well. It is not numerous, but look for it in mixed flocks of swallows over farmlands near Sohar and Salalah or at As Sayh in Musandam.

This blue and white swallow is easy to identify by its striking, white rump that can be seen in flight from a considerable distance. No other swallow in Oman has a white rump. The underparts are all white, too. Like other swallows it feeds by flying endlessly back and forth over grassy areas and other places where flying insects abound. It is less likely than other swallows to be seen resting on electrical wires.

Jan	Feb	Mar	Apr	May	Jun	Jul	Aug	Sep	Oct	Nov	Dec

Swallows and martins are excellent fliers. Included are the very common Barn Swallow and the not so common Red-rumped Swallow.

Barn Swallow

Hirundo rustica
19 cm

The Barn Swallow is an abundant passage migrant and also a common winter visitor. It may turn up anywhere it can find flying insects, especially on farmlands. Sometimes seen in huge flocks numbering several thousands.

The Barn Swallow is a bird of the air. It seems to fly endlessly in search of food and only rarely takes a rest on electrical wires or other suitable perches. Most often seen in loose flocks patrolling back and forth over grassy fields. The upperparts are dark, purplish-black all over. In autumn a good number of birds are juveniles lacking the long tail streamers. A pair once made an unsuccessful attempt to breed in Musandam.

| Jan | Feb | Mar | Apr | May | Jun | Jul | Aug | Sep | Oct | Nov | Dec |

Red-rumped Swallow

Cecropis daurica
18 cm

Though much less common than the previous species, the Red-rumped Swallow should be looked for in feeding flocks mixed with Barn Swallows, especially during spring migration. Likely areas are farmlands and coastal areas.

Red-rumped Swallows are relatively easy to pick out in a mixed flock of swallows. Whereas the Barn Swallow looks all dark above, the Red-rumped has a pale reddish rump as the name suggests. If a group of swallows is found on electrical wires, check for birds with a reddish crown and streaking on the breast. These will be Red-rumped Swallows. Never found in Oman in large numbers, but the odd bird is seen now and again.

Jan Feb Mar Apr May Jun Jul Aug Sep Oct Nov Dec

47

Wagtails are birds with long tails that are constantly moved up and down, hence their name. Four species are found in Oman.

Yellow Wagtail

Motacilla flava
17 cm

feldegg

beema

lutea

The Yellow Wagtail is an abundant passage migrant and winter visitor, commonest on farmlands in north and south Oman, but may turn up in several other habitats where insects are found. Al Qurm Natural Park, Al Ansab Lagoons and hotel gardens are other likely places to find this bird.

In general the Yellow Wagtail is yellow below and olive-green above. The head pattern varies considerably depending on the race. The most common races found in Oman are: *beema* (sometimes called 'Sykes's Wagtail'), *thunbergi*, *flava*, *feldegg* and *lutea*. Immature birds and winter adults of the different races look very similar, but spring males can often be identified to race. Large flocks usually contain several races.

| Jan | Feb | Mar | Apr | May | Jun | Jul | Aug | Sep | Oct | Nov | Dec |

Citrine Wagtail

Motacilla citreola
17 cm

autumn and winter

spring

The Citrine Wagtail is a common passage migrant and winter visitor, more widespread, but less numerous than the Yellow Wagtail. It is common on farmlands and wet areas. Look for it on farms on the Batinah and near Salalah and at Al Qurm Natural Park and Al Ansab Lagoons.

The Citrine Wagtail closely resembles the Yellow Wagtail except in spring when in its stunning breeding plumage. In autumn and winter look for a yellowish wagtail with a grey back, two clear, white wingbars and a dark patch on the cheek surrounded by yellow. The Citrine Wagtail is not found in huge flocks like the Yellow Wagtail. More often it is encountered singly or possibly a few birds together in areas where water is present.

Jan	Feb	Mar	Apr	May	Jun	Jul	Aug	Sep	Oct	Nov	Dec

Grey Wagtail

Motacilla cinerea
18 cm

The least numerous of the four wagtails and the most localized one. The most reliable place is Ayn Hamran east of Salalah from September to April. The small run-off stream through the wooded area always seems to hold one or two Grey Wagtails.

This bird has an very long tail which always seems to be wagging up and down. Whether the bird is sitting or foraging along a stream, the tail is never at rest. Other good identification marks are the grey head with a white supercilium, the grey back and no obvious wing bars. It has yellow underparts and a male in spring is a stunning bird. If disturbed the bird takes off for a short distance in an undulating flight.

| Jan | Feb | Mar | Apr | May | Jun | Jul | Aug | Sep | Oct | Nov | Dec |

White Wagtail

Motacilla alba
17 cm

spring

autumn

personata
in spring

The most numerous and widespread of the wagtails. The White Wagtail can be found in a variety of habitats, from farmlands and parks to lakes and coastal lagoons. Difficult to miss on farmlands on the Batinah and near Salalah or at Al Ansab Lagoons and Al Qurm Natural Park.

The White Wagtail is a black, grey and white bird throughout the year. In winter it can look rather dull, but in spring the head pattern is unmistakable. A few visiting birds belong to the race *personata* (often called Masked Wagtail) from central Asia. It has extensive black on the head and only a small white area around the eye. White Wagtails are sometimes seen in massive flocks containing thousands of birds coming to roost sites.

| Jan | Feb | Mar | Apr | May | Jun | Jul | Aug | Sep | Oct | Nov | Dec |

Pipits are close relatives of wagtails (previous pages), but they are much less brightly coloured, all being brownish-grey with some streaking and therefore more difficult to identify correctly.

Tawny Pipit

Anthus campestris
18 cm

The Tawny Pipit is the most common pipit in Oman. It is abundant on farmlands during passage and in winter. Look for it on farms near Sohar and Salalah as well as farms in the interior, such as Mabr Farm near Hayma and Al Balid Farm north of Thumrayt.

The Tawny Pipit is a large pipit, always found walking on the open ground, it does not sit in trees and bushes. Though many Tawny Pipits can be found on one farm, they are not seen in flocks, rather many individuals over a large area. Good identification features for this pipit are the size, lack of heavy streaking on the breast and a neat row of brown feather centres on the folded wing. With practice the call is useful as well.

Jan	Feb	Mar	Apr	May	Jun	Jul	Aug	Sep	Oct	Nov	Dec

Water Pipit

Anthus spinoletta
16 cm

The Water Pipit is a fairly common winter visitor on farmlands arriving late in autumn and leaving early in spring. It is most common at Sun Farms near Sohar, but can also be found at farms near Salalah and in the interior desert at Qatbit oasis and Muntasar.

Pipits, like wagtails, walk - they don't hop like sparrows. The Water Pipit is a smaller bird than the Tawny Pipit and has a relatively shorter tail. It is the only pipit in Oman with black legs. As the name suggests, it favours wet areas: permanent pools in the desert and grasslands where irrigation leaves standing water on a regular basis. Not normally seen in large flocks. Individual birds may be seen dashing about trying to catch insects.

| Jan | Feb | Mar | Apr | May | Jun | Jul | Aug | Sep | Oct | Nov | Dec |

These two pipits look rather similar, except in spring when the Red-throated Pipit is unique. The extent of streaking on the breast and flanks are good identification features to look for.

Red-throated Pipit

Anthus cervinus
15 cm

autumn & winter

spring

A common passage migrant in spring and autumn and a fairly common winter visitor. Good places to look for this bird are farmlands in north and south Oman and - particularly during spring migration in April - on As Sayh in Musandam.

As with other pipits, the male and female look the same. Only in spring does the Red-throated Pipit have a reddish throat and is then unmistakable. In autumn and winter the bird is heavily streaked on the breast with bold streaking continuing onto the flanks. Also the back is streaked. This is the most heavily streaked pipit, making it look rather dark from a distance. Sometimes seen in flocks with a hundred birds or more.

| Jan | Feb | Mar | Apr | May | Jun | Jul | Aug | Sep | Oct | Nov | Dec |

Tree Pipit

Anthus trivialis
15 cm

A fairly common passage migrant and less common winter visitor. Tree Pipits may be encountered anywhere there are trees. The largest number (80) was recorded at Hilf on Masirah. More often seen in very small numbers.

Tree Pipits look very similar to Red-throated Pipits, but the streaking is less heavy, especially on the flanks. The basic colour of the Tree Pipit is warmer than the other pipits. In autumn, it is an early passage migrant with good numbers in September and October before the main arrival of the Red-throated Pipits. Unlike the other pipits, Tree Pipits often perch in trees, but they can also be seen walking on the ground.

Jan Feb Mar Apr May Jun Jul Aug Sep Oct Nov Dec

Redstarts are basically black and rufous birds. When landing on a branch they shiver the tail a second or two, a good identification mark.

Black Redstart

Phoenicurus ochruros
15 cm

Male

Female

A widespread and common winter visitor and can be found wherever there are trees. Good places to look for this bird are the Sayq Plateau, the woodlands at Khatmat Milahah just south of the UAE border and the foothill parks near Salalah such as Ayn Razat and Ayn Hamran.

The races of Black Redstart wintering in Oman have extensive rufous underparts. Thus care has to be exercised when identifying Black Redstarts especially during spring and autumn migration when Black and Common Redstarts may overlap. Note the extent of black on the breast of the male Black Redstart compared to the male Common Redstart. The female Black Redstart is darker than the female Common Redstart.

| Jan | Feb | Mar | Apr | May | Jun | Jul | Aug | Sep | Oct | Nov | Dec |

Common Redstart

Phoenicurus phoenicurus
15 cm

Male

Despite the name, the Common Redstart is much less common and more localized in Oman than the Black Redstart. It is common only in Musandam (Sall Ala, As Sayh and Ar Rawdah) in April when dozens can be seen.

The main spring passage of Common Redstarts follows the departure of Black Redstarts, making identification easier, except in April when the two species may occur together. Look for the less extensive black on the breast and the white forehead of the male Common Redstart. The habit of both redstarts is the same: they sit quietly on a branch, often in the shade, fly to the ground for a larvae and return to the branch shivering the tail.

Jan	Feb	Mar	Apr	May	Jun	Jul	Aug	Sep	Oct	Nov	Dec

Wheatears are small passerines of the open country. In general, they have a characteristic tail pattern with a black center and tip and white sides such that the black area forms an inverted "T", The Desert Wheatear, however, has an all-black tail.

Isabelline Wheatear

Oenanthe isabellina
16 cm

The Isabelline Wheatear is an abundant passage migrant and winter visitor to farmlands and other open, arid country all over Oman, but especially at farms near Sohar and Salalah and at As Sayh in Musandam where dozens may be encountered.

The best field character of this wheatear is the overall uniform sandy colour with little or no black markings on the wings. The lore (a line between the eye and the bill) is black. The posture is upright, sleek and elegant. Always found on the ground, but may perch on a small rock to get a better view of the surrounding landscape. Runs frequently after prey. Horizontal when running, but regains upright stance upon stopping.

Jan	Feb	Mar	Apr	May	Jun	Jul	Aug	Sep	Oct	Nov	Dec

Desert Wheatear

Oenanthe deserti
15 cm

Male

Female

In winter the most common and widespread of the 14 species of wheatears found in Oman. The wide range of habitats include farmlands, deserts, coastal dunes and even beaches. Curiously, males far outnumber females during winter in Oman.

The handsome male Desert Wheatear is distinctive with its black face mask connecting with a broad black line on the wings when the bird is perched. The tail is all black unlike other wheatears. The female resembles an Isabelline Wheatear, but has more blackish markings on the wing. At home on the ground, but will also perch in bushes from where it keeps an eye open for prey below, especially caterpillars.

| Jan | Feb | Mar | Apr | May | Jun | Jul | Aug | Sep | Oct | Nov | Dec |

Flycatchers are small insect-eating passerines. They eat flying insects caught on the wing.

Spotted Flycatcher

Muscicapa striata
14 cm

The Spotted Flycatcher is an abundant passage migrant in spring and autumn wherever there are trees and bushes. Large concentrations are found during the short spring migration in the gardens at desert motels at Al Ghaftayn and Qatbit as well as the Dhofar foothills.

A plain-looking small bird but a joy to watch in action. Patience is part of its character and it may sit for long periods on a branch, often in the shade. With insects around, however, the hunt is on. With quick twists and turns in the air the pursuit goes on until a meal is secured. Also comes to the ground looking for caterpillars. Good identification characteristics of this bird include the stripy forehead and faint streaking on the breast.

| Jan | Feb | Mar | Apr | May | Jun | Jul | Aug | Sep | Oct | Nov | Dec |

Shrikes are medium-sized birds sometimes called butcherbirds because they have the habit of impaling their prey - insects, small lizards, even smaller birds - on a thorn or other sharp object to tear the prey apart.

Isabelline Shrike

Lanius isabellinus
19 cm

Turkestan Shrike

The Isabelline Shrike is an abundant passage migrant and winter visitor all over the country. It is particularly common during the autumn passage and found wherever there are trees and bushes. Like other shrikes it has a powerful bill used when tearing prey apart.

The name of this bird refers to its overall pale sandy-brown colour. A dark line through the eye gives it an aggressive look, quite appropriate for its nature. The tail is rufous and there is a white mark in the wing best seen when the bird is in flight. It may sit quietly on a branch on the lookout for prey on the ground below. A more strikingly looking race, referred to as 'Turkestan Shrike,' is common during spring and autumn migration.

| Jan | Feb | Mar | Apr | May | Jun | Jul | Aug | Sep | Oct | Nov | Dec |

The two grey shrikes in Oman are very similar in plumage and behaviour and have only recently been split into separate species.

Southern Grey Shrike   *Lanius meridionalis aucheri*
25 cm

The Southern Grey Shrike is an abundant breeding resident over most of the country and found in a wide variety of habitats: parks, woodlands, mountains and deserts. Look for it on farmlands near Sohar and Salalah as well as in open, arid areas with scattered trees.

This bird can be identified by its grey plumage and extensive black face mask with a narrow, black line above the black bill. The breeding season in Oman is late winter. It is an aggressive and fearless bird. Once we witnessed a Southern Grey Shrike attack and kill a sand viper. As the dead snake was too heavy for the shrike to carry, it simply cut the snake in half with its sharp bill and flew off with one half.

| Jan | Feb | Mar | Apr | May | Jun | Jul | Aug | Sep | Oct | Nov | Dec |

Steppe Grey Shrike

Lanius (m.) pallidirostris
25 cm

A fairly common passage migrant and winter visitor, but much less numerous than the previous species. Look for it in similar habitats, especially on farmlands near Sohar and Salalah. Usually seen singly and never in groups.

The Steppe Grey Shrike is a much sought after bird by visiting birdwatchers. Skill is needed to identify this species. It is paler than the Southern Grey Shrike, has a paler bill, pale lores and a pale forehead. It is an equally aggressive bird that will attack prey almost as large as itself. Like the Southern Grey Shrike it will impale its prey on a thorn in order to pull it apart into manageable mouthfuls.

Jan Feb Mar Apr May Jun Jul Aug Sep Oct Nov Dec

These two shrikes are not as common and are more restricted in their choice of habitat than the previous two species.

Woodchat Shrike

Lanius senator
18 cm

The Woodchat Shrike is a fairly common spring **passage** migrant in Musandam, but much less regularly found during autumn or in other places in Oman. The best places to look for it are Khatmat Milahah and Musandam in March and April.

The Woodchat Shrike is found in open woodlands, parks and farmlands with scattered trees. It is readily identified by its rufous crown and nape bordered with black. It has white wing panels, throat and underparts. The tail is black. Like other shrikes it perches in a tree or on a pole surveying the ground below for prey. It feeds mostly on caterpillars and large insects. Usually silent while in Oman.

| Jan | Feb | Mar | Apr | May | Jun | Jul | Aug | Sep | Oct | Nov | Dec |

Masked Shrike

Lanius nubicus
18 cm

The Masked Shrike is even less common than the Woodchat Shrike, but regularly found in Musandam in spring. Less regular in autumn and during winter. Qatbit Motel and Ayn Hamran are other sites where Masked Shrikes turn up with some regularity.

The Masked Shrike is found in wooded areas. Often hiding in a bush, or sitting on a branch in the shade, it can be hard to see. Once found, it is easy to identify by its black and creamy-white plumage. The adult male in breeding plumage has a rufous touch to the flanks. Usually seen singly, though up to six birds have been seen spread out over a relatively small area of Bukha in Musandam.

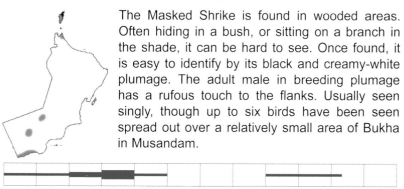

| Jan | Feb | Mar | Apr | May | Jun | Jul | Aug | Sep | Oct | Nov | Dec |

Two common, resident birds that are found over much of the country.

Arabian Babbler

Turdoides squamiceps
26 cm

The Arabian Babbler is most common in northern Oman and Musandam, less common in southern Oman and absent from Masirah. Normally quite easy to find at Al Qurm Natural Park, in the woodlands at Khatmat Milahah and at Sall Ala in Musandam.

The Arabian Babbler is a rather large bird with a long tail and a large down-curved bill. It is uniform brownish-grey in colour. Found in family parties of 5-10 birds where there are dense bushes and trees. One bird will sit high in a tree keeping watch while the rest of the party forages on the ground. If danger is detected, the bird on watch duty sounds the alarm call, a high pitched whistle, and the whole party moves off to a safer place.

Jan	Feb	Mar	Apr	May	Jun	Jul	Aug	Sep	Oct	Nov	Dec

Chestnut-bellied Sandgrouse

Pterocles exustus
32 cm

Female

Males

The Chestnut-bellied Sandgrouse is a common and widespread resident over most of the country. Look for it coming to drink during mid-morning at Al Ansab Lagoons near Muscat and at Sun Farms near Sohar.

One of four common sandgrouse species found in Oman. This one is common on farmlands while the others are typical desert birds (see *Mountains and Deserts* section, p 193). The male has a long pointed tail and is easy to recognize by his black band on the lower breast while the female - like other female sandgrouse - is more subtle in colour but still with a demarcating line separating the breast and the belly feathers.

Jan	Feb	Mar	Apr	May	Jun	Jul	Aug	Sep	Oct	Nov	Dec

67

These two visitors are easy to identify based on their plumage and their habits, but patience may be needed to locate the Bluethroat.

Rufous-tailed Scrub Robin *Cercotrichas galactotes*
15 cm

This abundant passage migrant is seen both spring and autumn. It may turn up anywhere there are some trees. Easy to find in late April and early May in Al Qurm Natural Park, Khatmat Milahah, the resthouses along the Muscat - Salalah road and in parks near Salalah.

This is a conspicuous bird often seen out in the open near a tree. It slowly raises and lowers the rufous tail, runs for a bit and repeats the procedure. While the tail is up, it may be fanned to reveal the dark tip with the white corners. The wings are lowered and while stopping for a moment the wings are flicked. A black eye-line and a white supercilium complete the obvious identification characteristics of this species.

| Jan | Feb | Mar | Apr | May | Jun | Jul | Aug | Sep | Oct | Nov | Dec |

Bluethroat

Luscinia svecica
14 cm

Female

Male

A common passage migrant and winter visitor to farmlands, parks and gardens where there is moist undergrowth. Look for it at Al Qurm Natural Park, at the hotel gardens in Muscat, at Sun Farms near Sohar and the parks, gardens and reed-fringed lagoons near Salalah.

The Bluethroat is a skulker spending most of its time hidden away in the thick vegetation, but a brief sighting may be had as the bird suddenly appears at the edge of a thicket. The adult male retains a bit of blue on his upper breast during winter. The immature male and the female may not have any blue at all, but will at least have a blackish 'necklace.' Another good identification feature are the rufous sides at the base of the tail.

| Jan | Feb | Mar | Apr | May | Jun | Jul | Aug | Sep | Oct | Nov | Dec |

These two species of starlings are regularly found in Oman, but neither is particularly common. Starlings walk on the ground rather than hop.

Common Starling

Sturnus vulgaris
20 cm

Despite being called Common Starling and being one of the most familiar birds in Europe, this species is not so common in Oman. Likely places to find it include hotel gardens near Muscat and farmlands near Sohar and Salalah.

In summer the Starling sports a beautiful dark plumage with a greenish and purplish metallic sheen. While in Oman, however, it looks quite different, being all dark with numerous white specks as a result of white feather tips. Most often seen in small, noisy flocks feeding on lawns or grassy fields, sometimes in the company of Rose-coloured Starlings and, especially in the north, Common Mynas (p 26).

Jan	Feb	Mar	Apr	May	Jun	Jul	Aug	Sep	Oct	Nov	Dec

Rose-coloured Starling

Pastor roseus
20 cm

The Rose-coloured Starling is a fairly common passage migrant and winter visitor, but rather localized. Most sightings are from Sun Farms in Sohar, Al Balid Farm near Thumrayt and, particularly, Jarziz Farm and Sahnawt Farm in Salalah.

The Rose-coloured Starling is an easy bird to identify by its black and rosy plumage. Young birds and birds seen during autumn and early winter will have the pink replaced by a sandy brown colour, but in the same pattern as on the spring birds. Sometimes the species is found in quite large groups with up to 200 seen together near Salalah. In the north, a feeding flock of starlings may be a mixture of several starling species.

| Jan | Feb | Mar | Apr | May | Jun | Jul | Aug | Sep | Oct | Nov | Dec |

Siberian Stonechat

Saxicola maurus
12 cm

The Siberian Stonechat is a fairly common passage migrant and winter visitor to parks and farmlands throughout the country. Good places to look for it are As Sayh in Musandam, Sun Farms near Sohar, Al Balid Farm north of Thumrayt and the farms in Salalah.

This small passerine is easy to identify by its black head, rufous breast and white-sided neck. The Black Redstart (p 56) is also found in winter in similar habitats but is longer-tailed and does not have the white neck markings. The Siberian Stonechat sits conspicuously on a pole or on the top of a weed on the lookout for insects. If prey is spotted on the ground below, the bird dashes down and returns to the same or a nearby post.

| Jan | Feb | Mar | Apr | May | Jun | Jul | Aug | Sep | Oct | Nov | Dec |

Warblers are among the most challenging birds to identify. It is often difficult to get good views as they hide in the middle of a tree. Only the most common species are covered here.

Eastern Olivaceous Warbler

Iduna pallida
13 cm

The Eastern Olivaceous Warbler is a common passage migrant in spring and autumn, found wherever there are trees. It can be quite numerous at peak migration times in Al Qurm Natural Park and at the resthouses along the Muscat - Salalah road.

The Eastern Olivaceous Warbler is one of those 'LBJs' (little brown jobs) that can be difficult to identify. Basically, it has uniformly olive-greyish upperparts and paler underparts with no conspicuous identification features. It has a slanting forehead giving the impression that the head is longish. The bird spends much of the daylight hours foraging in trees and bushes looking for insects. It does not come onto the ground.

Jan	Feb	Mar	Apr	May	Jun	Jul	Aug	Sep	Oct	Nov	Dec

Two Phylloscopus warblers closely related and difficult to tell apart in the field. Look for the difference in leg colour!

Common Chiffchaff

Phylloscopus collybita
11 cm

The Common Chiffchaff is a common passage migrant and winter visitor to areas with trees. Particularly common in the desert in areas such as Muntasar, Qatbit Motel garden and farmlands, but also found in gardens and parks throughout the country.

Great care is needed to separate the Common Chiffchaff from the Willow Warbler. Both are rather non-descript small warblers. Both are very active looking for food as they move about in trees. With good views, the black legs of the Chiffchaff are a good field mark. In late winter and early spring the Common Chiffchaff becomes quite vocal and sings its own name: 'chiff-chaff chiff-chaff' and identification is straightforward.

| Jan | Feb | Mar | Apr | May | Jun | Jul | Aug | Sep | Oct | Nov | Dec |

Willow Warbler

Phylloscopus trochilus
11 cm

The Willow Warbler is a fairly common passage migrant in spring and autumn. The most reliable place to find this species is Musandam in April when up to 200 birds have been recorded, but Willow Warblers may turn up anywhere there are trees and bushes.

Good identification features of this species are the overall olive-green plumage, pale yellow super-cilium, pale legs (black in Common Chiffchaff), and lack of wing bars. While in Oman the Willow Warbler is usually silent. Unlike the Common Chiffchaff, the Willow Warbler often comes to the ground looking for food. Notice also that the arrival of the Willow Warbler in spring follows the main departure of the Common Chiffchaff.

| Jan | Feb | Mar | Apr | May | Jun | Jul | Aug | Sep | Oct | Nov | Dec |

These two whitethroats are the most common Sylvia *warblers found in Oman and should not be difficult to tell apart.*

Desert Whitethroat

Sylvia minula
12 cm

The Desert Whitethroat is a very common passage migrant and winter visitor. It can be found anywhere there are trees and bushes: gardens, parks, wadis - from the coast to the mountains. Particularly common in Musandam, at Khatmat Milahah and at the desert oases.

The Desert Whitethroat is a small, greyish warbler with a darkish ear patch and a pale throat. Obtaining good views may not be so easy as the bird often hides in the densest part of the foliage. Rather vocal and, with practice, easy to identify on its call: 'tsi tsi-tsi.' Always stays high in the trees and bushes and rarely comes to the ground. More widespread and found over a longer period than the Common Whitethroat.

| Jan | Feb | Mar | Apr | May | Jun | Jul | Aug | Sep | Oct | Nov | Dec |

Common Whitethroat

Sylvia communis
14 cm

The Common Whitethroat is a common passage migrant in spring and autumn, but very rare during winter. Good places to look for this bird are parks and gardens in Muscat and Salalah as well as desert oases such as Muntasar and Qatbit.

The Common Whitethroat is quite a bit bigger than the Desert Whitethroat. Combined with the white throat, the red wing panel (actually rufous edges to the wing feathers) will aid in identification. The main diet is insects, but Common Whitethroats will also eat dates if some are left on the palm trees when the birds pass through Oman on their autumn migration. Much less vocal than the previous species.

| Jan | Feb | Mar | Apr | May | Jun | Jul | Aug | Sep | Oct | Nov | Dec |

These two small, ground-dwelling birds are both migratory and more common in spring than in autumn.

Ortolan Bunting

Emberiza hortulana
16 cm

The Ortolan Bunting is a fairly common passage migrant, especially in spring. Though birds can turn up just about anywhere, the easiest place to find them is at As Sayh and - to a lesser extent - Sall Ala and Ar Rawdah, all in Musandam.

Ortolan Buntings are normally encountered in small groups on a grassy field, sometimes mixed with small birds such as other buntings and pipits. The birds move slowly through the grass looking for seeds. The male has an olive-green head with an L-shaped yellow line from the bill bordering the cheeks which is a good identification feature. Females and young birds generally show the same markings, but are much duller.

Jan	Feb	Mar	Apr	May	Jun	Jul	Aug	Sep	Oct	Nov	Dec

Black-headed Bunting

Emberiza melanocephala
17 cm

The Black-headed Bunting is a fairly common passage migrant in spring. Most records are from Musandam in April when over 100 birds have been seen on several occasions. Flocks of buntings should be studied carefully as several species often mix during migration.

The spring male is unmistakable with his black head and yellow underparts. Females and autumn males are very tricky to identify and look like several other non-descript, small birds. In spring, females can be identified and studied when in company with the handsome males. Black-headed Buntings are most often seen in small groups on the ground where they are looking for seeds.

| Jan | Feb | Mar | Apr | May | Jun | Jul | Aug | Sep | Oct | Nov | Dec |

79

These two relatively large passage migrants are somewhat similar in plumage, but have quite different habits.

Common Cuckoo

Cuculus canorus
33 cm

The Common Cuckoo is a fairly common passage migrant both spring and autumn. It may turn up anywhere in Oman where there are some trees and bushes. Regular places include Al Qurm Natural Park, hotel gardens near Muscat and at As Sayh in Musandam.

The Common Cuckoo may be common and familiar in Europe, but it is not so easy to find in Oman. It is a bird you just come across once in a while without really looking for it. In flight, the long tail, grey upperparts and striped underparts give this bird a strong resemblance to a Eurasian Sparrowhawk (p 96). The familiar call 'cuck-coo cuck-coo' is only heard in Musandam in April and May where a few birds may occasionally breed.

| Jan | Feb | Mar | Apr | May | Jun | Jul | Aug | Sep | Oct | Nov | Dec |

European Nightjar

Caprimulgus europaeus
26 cm

Female

A fairly common passage migrant, but not easy to find because of its secretive behaviour. To find it, try walking around the trees at Muntasar, Dawkah or Qatbit Motel at the right time of the year. You may be lucky to come upon a nightjar or two.

The European Nightjar has a cryptic colouration making it difficult to spot when it sits quietly on a branch or on the ground against the trunk of a tree. It is active at night flying silently around trees and bushes scooping up insects. The bill is small, but the gape is enormous. The male has a conspicuous white spot on the wing and on the side of the tail tip. These spots are absent in the female.

Jan	Feb	Mar	Apr	May	Jun	Jul	Aug	Sep	Oct	Nov	Dec

Two more visitors that can be tricky to locate, especially the Wryneck with its cryptic colours.

Eurasian Wryneck

Jynx torquilla
16 cm

The Eurasian Wryneck is a fairly common passage migrant and winter visitor and may be found wherever there are trees. Good places are parks and gardens such as Al Qurm Natural Park, Hilf, Qatbit Motel, Ayn Hamran and Ayn Razat.

The Eurasian Wryneck is the only member of the woodpecker family found in Oman. Its name refers to its ability to turn its head 180 degrees. With such cryptic plumage it can be difficult to spot against the trunk or branch of a tree. Though it likes trees it may be seen on the ground near an ant nest licking up the inhabitants with its sticky tongue. Normally seen singly though ten were once recorded in a garden on Masirah.

| Jan | Feb | Mar | Apr | May | Jun | Jul | Aug | Sep | Oct | Nov | Dec |

Eurasian Golden Oriole

Oriolus oriolus
24 cm

Male

The Eurasian Golden Oriole is a fairly common autumn passage migrant, but rare on spring passage. Good places to look for it include parks and gardens as well as desert oases such as Muntasar, Qatbit Motel garden and Dawkah.

The adult male Eurasian Golden Oriole is a brilliantly yellow and black bird that cannot be mistaken for any other species. Young males and females that predominate on the autumn passage are olive-yellow in colour. Despite their bright colours, Eurasian Golden Orioles can be difficult to spot in the dense foliage of a tree. More likely is a glimpse of a large, yellowish bird flying away occasionally giving a harsh call.

| Jan | Feb | Mar | Apr | May | Jun | Jul | Aug | Sep | Oct | Nov | Dec |

83

These two lapwings are fairly large waders found on inland fields and wetlands, but not at the coast.

Red-wattled Lapwing

Vanellus indicus
32 cm

The Red-wattled Lapwing is a common breeding resident in northern Oman. It is easy to find at Al Qurm Natural Park, Al Ansab Lagoons and on farmlands on the Batinah coast. Gardens with large lawns may also have a pair of these birds.

The Red-wattled Lapwing is easy to identify both on its black-and-white head pattern and the red skin in front of the eyes. It is usually found not far away from water and is likely to be heard before it is seen. If you enter the territory of a pair, one or both birds will fly up and start calling 'did-he-do-it, did-he-do-it,' an easy call to recognize. During courtship the birds make aerial displays - even at night - giving the same calls.

| Jan | Feb | Mar | Apr | May | Jun | Jul | Aug | Sep | Oct | Nov | Dec |

White-tailed Lapwing

Vanellus leucurus
28 cm

The White-tailed Lapwing is a common, but very localized, passage migrant and winter visitor, mostly to north Oman. The best places to look for it are Al Qurm Natural Park, Al Ansab Lagoons and Sun Farms, Sohar, with a possibility also at Khawr Taqah in south Oman.

This plover is less colourful than the previous one, but is still easy to recognize with its bright yellow legs and uniform, greyish upperparts. In flight it shows conspicuous black and white wings and a pure white tail with the long legs protruding well beyond the tail. The White-tailed Lapwing has a much softer call than the Red-wattled Lapwing. It is almost always found near water, usually a few together, but never in large flocks.

Jan	Feb	Mar	Apr	May	Jun	Jul	Aug	Sep	Oct	Nov	Dec

Pacific Golden Plover

Pluvialis fulva
24 cm

Breeding
plumage

Non-breeding
plumage

The Pacific Golden Plover is a common passage migrant and winter
visitor. For several years running about a dozen birds have wintered
at Al Qurm Natural Park. Other likely places include farmlands in both
north and south Oman.

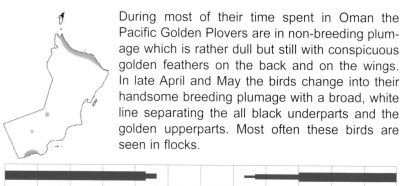

During most of their time spent in Oman the
Pacific Golden Plovers are in non-breeding plumage which is rather dull but still with conspicuous
golden feathers on the back and on the wings.
In late April and May the birds change into their
handsome breeding plumage with a broad, white
line separating the all black underparts and the
golden upperparts. Most often these birds are
seen in flocks.

| Jan | Feb | Mar | Apr | May | Jun | Jul | Aug | Sep | Oct | Nov | Dec |

While this species is found at inland pools and farmlands, its close relatives, the Common Ringed and the Kentish Plover are found at the coast.

Little Ringed Plover

Charadrius dubius
15 cm

Non-breeding plumage

Breeding plumage

The Little Ringed Plover is an abundant passage migrant and winter visitor mainly to farmlands in north and south Oman. A few birds stay over summer to breed, for example at Sun Farms near Sohar and Al Qurm Natural Park near Muscat.

This is a much smaller plover than the previous species. In breeding plumage from March to June the Little Ringed Plover is easy to recognize on it bright yellow eye-ring in addition to the dark breast-band. At other times it looks very similar to the Common Ringed Plover (p 120), but still has a bit of yellow around the eye and paler legs than that species. In flight, the Little Ringed Plover does not show a white wing bar unlike the Common Ringed Plover.

| Jan | Feb | Mar | Apr | May | Jun | Jul | Aug | Sep | Oct | Nov | Dec |

Though both these two species belong to the shorebird or wader family, the Collared Pratincole looks more like a tern than a wader.

Collared Pratincole

Glareola pratincola
25 cm

The Collared Pratincole is a fairly common passage migrant and an uncommon winter visitor. Recently a colony of birds have established a breeding territory at Sun Farms near Sohar, probably the only place in Arabia where they breed.

With its short legs, forked tail and long pointed wings, the Collared Pratincole resembles a tern. Even in flight the silhouette is more of a tern than of a shorebird. This species, however, is easy to recognize on its black 'necklace' from eye to eye and, in flight, the white rump. If the light is good the red underwings and the white, trailing edge to the wings are excellent field characters. It favours barren fields where it blends in perfectly.

| Jan | Feb | Mar | Apr | May | Jun | Jul | Aug | Sep | Oct | Nov | Dec |

Ruff

Philomachus pugnax
Female 22, male 28 cm

The Ruff is an abundant passage migrant and winter visitor. It may be found near ponds and lagoons, but it is most common on farmlands all over the country. Sizeable flocks numbering several hundred birds have been encountered.

The Ruff gets its name from a collar of ruffed-up feathers on male birds in breeding plumage. While in Oman these ruffs are not present, however, and the Ruff is a rather nondescript bird. Good field marks are the smallish head with short bill and the checkered upperparts. Legs are long and orange in colour. In flight, a horseshoe-shaped white patch is visible on the rump. Males are considerably bigger than females.

Jan	Feb	Mar	Apr	May	Jun	Jul	Aug	Sep	Oct	Nov	Dec

These two species are long-legged birds of farmlands with grassy fields. Cattle Egrets may also turn up on lawns and even roundabouts.

Cattle Egret

Bubulcus ibis
50 cm

This species is a common winter visitor and numbers seem to be increasing. A few birds may stay over summer. Impossible to miss at Sun Farms, Sohar. Also common on farms near Salalah and sometimes also at Al Qurm Natural Park near Muscat.

The Cattle Egret is a small heron that can be separated from the other white herons by its short, yellow bill and, in spring, some buff-coloured feathers on the crown and breast. Leg colour varies from yellow in spring to black in autumn. Large flocks numbering up to 200 birds roam around large farms frequenting the cow pens and the fields where grass is being cut for fodder. Grasshoppers form a major part of their diet.

| Jan | Feb | Mar | Apr | May | Jun | Jul | Aug | Sep | Oct | Nov | Dec |

White Stork

Ciconia ciconia
100 cm

The White Stork is a common autumn passage migrant with many birds staying over winter, especially in southern Oman. Flocks may regularly be encountered on farms near Sohar and Salalah as well as at the waste disposal site near Raysut west of Salalah.

A familiar bird in European folklore, the White Stork is unmistakable with its black and white plumage and bright red bill and legs. In flight, it might be confused with an adult Egyptian Vulture, but the long legs and neck of the stork easily set the two species apart. On farmlands the White Stork walks around grassy fields, especially areas with newly cut grass, looking for grasshoppers. A gregarious bird that is often found in large flocks.

| Jan | Feb | Mar | Apr | May | Jun | Jul | Aug | Sep | Oct | Nov | Dec |

In addition to the abundant Marsh Harrier of lakes and lagoons (p 171) there are two common harriers, both found on farmlands in Oman.

Pallid Harrier

Circus macrourus
44 cm

Male

Female

The Pallid Harrier is a common passage migrant and winter visitor. Most commonly found on farmlands in both north and south Oman, but also seen regularly in desert oases such as Muntasar, Qatbit and Dawkah.

The adult male is a handsome bird, very pale grey all over except for a black wedge of primary flight feathers. Immature birds and females are mostly brown with a white rump that is conspicuous in flight. Identifying these from the very similar immature and female Montagu's Harrier requires patience and experience. The best mark of the Pallid Harrier is a white line behind a dark line on the cheek.

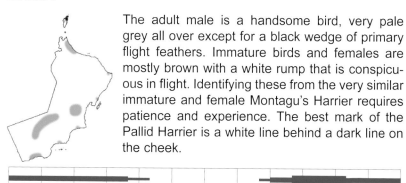

| Jan | Feb | Mar | Apr | May | Jun | Jul | Aug | Sep | Oct | Nov | Dec |

Montagu's Harrier

Circus pygargus
45 cm

Males

Female

The Montagu's Harrier is a common passage migrant and winter visitor, slightly more common than the Pallid Harrier. The most regular habitat is farmlands such as Sun Farms near Sohar, Al Balid Farm north of Thumrayt and the farms near Salalah.

Adult males are darker grey than male Pallid Harriers with more extensive black in the wing tips and a narrow black line on the secondaries. Females and immature birds are very similar to Pallid Harriers, but lack the extra white line in the face. Firm identification of female and immature Pallid and Montagu's Harriers can be difficult and these birds are often just referred to as 'Ringtails' even by experienced birdwatchers.

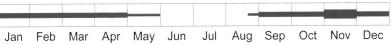

| Jan | Feb | Mar | Apr | May | Jun | Jul | Aug | Sep | Oct | Nov | Dec |

Two species of kestrels are found in Oman. They are very similar and skill is required for a firm identification.

Lesser Kestrel

Falco naumanni
30 cm

Males

Female

The Lesser Kestrel is a globally endangered species. In Oman it is a fairly common spring passage migrant on farmlands with grassy fields on Al Batinah, in Musandam and near Salalah. Over 100 birds have been seen together.

Separating Lesser from Common Kestrels can be tricky. The adult male Lesser Kestrel has a grey panel on the upperwing and fewer black spots on both upperside and underside compared with the adult male Common Kestrel. Females of the two species are reddish-brown and heavily streaked black above and are virtually identical. Habitat, behaviour and the time of year give important clues as to the identity of these birds.

Jan	Feb	Mar	Apr	May	Jun	Jul	Aug	Sep	Oct	Nov	Dec

Common Kestrel

Falco tinnunculus
34 cm

Females

Male

The Common Kestrel is an abundant passage migrant and winter visitor in Oman with a few pairs staying year-round to breed in the mountains and on coastal cliffs. During the cooler months, however, these birds are most common on farmlands, in large parks and gardens.

The adult male can be separated from the very similar Lesser Kestrel by its reddish upperparts with numerous black spots, but lacking a broad grey panel. Females of the two species are almost identical. At close range, Common Kestrels can be seen to have black claws while Lesser Kestrels have white claws. In addition, Common Kestrels are not normally seen in flocks, but found either singly or as a breeding pair.

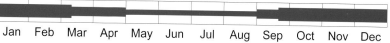

Jan   Feb   Mar   Apr   May   Jun   Jul   Aug   Sep   Oct   Nov   Dec

Eurasian Sparrowhawk

Accipiter nisus
28-38 cm

Eurasian Collared Dove

The Eurasian Sparrowhawk is a common passage migrant and winter visitor. It is most common in large parks and on farmlands especially where trees are present. Normally seen singly though up to four have been seen in the same area.

The Eurasian Sparrowhawk is usually encountered by chance as the bird flies high in the air or shoots over a field at high speed in hot pursuit of a potential meal: birds up to the size of doves. The upperparts are dark grey, underparts pale with numerous, horizontal bars. Females are larger than males. In flight the silhouette resembles that of a Common Cuckoo (p 80), but the head is larger and the bill more powerful.

| Jan | Feb | Mar | Apr | May | Jun | Jul | Aug | Sep | Oct | Nov | Dec |

Birds at the coast

This section deals with common birds found at the open beaches, off-shore islands and mangrove creeks. A few pelagic species that rarely, if ever, set their feet on land in Oman are included as well.

The birds selected include most of the gulls and terns found in Oman as well as many shorebirds or waders seen on sandy beaches or tidal mudflats.

Some species from other parts of this book, particularly birds of coastal lagoons, can be common also at the beach. If you cannot find a species you have seen at the beach in this section, check out the following:

Western Reef Heron, p 147
Grey Heron, p 146
Little Egret, p 148
Western Great Egret, p 149
Eurasian Spoonbill, p 155
Greater Flamingo, p 157
Pied Avocet, p 177
Little Stint, p 178
Common Redshank, p 182
Common Greenshank, p 184

Western Marsh Harrier, p 171
Pallid Harrier, p 92
Common Kestrel, p 95
Egyptian Vulture, p 194
Rock Dove, p 207
Desert Wheatear, p 59
Crested Lark, p 38
Barn Swallow, p 46
White Wagtail, p 51
Fan-tailed Raven, p 234

Swift Tern

Gulls and terns are the most numerous birds at the beach. Gulls can be told from terns in that the latter plunge-dive for their food.

Sooty Gull

Larus hemprichii
45 cm

The Sooty Gull is an abundant breeding resident on offshore islands. Outside the breeding season (July - October) these birds gather in huge numbers on beaches all along the Omani coastline. This is the most common gull found in Oman.

No other gull regularly seen in Oman has an over-all sooty-brown plumage. In breeding plumage the Sooty Gull has white markings on the neck and a colourful bill. Immature birds are dark grey all over unlike immatures of other gulls that are brownish and stripy. The Sooty Gull is a familiar bird along the whole coastline of Oman with hundreds or even thousands gathering near fishing villages.

| Jan | Feb | Mar | Apr | May | Jun | Jul | Aug | Sep | Oct | Nov | Dec |

Slender-billed Gull
Chroicocephalus genei
43 cm

The Slender-billed Gull is an abundant winter visitor to sandy beaches throughout Oman. Particularly common on the east coast from Ras Al Hadd to Ad Duqm as well as on Masirah. Flocks up to 50,000 birds have been estimated at Barr Al Hikman.

This gull is much smaller than the following two species that also have white heads. The Slender-billed Gull in winter may be confused with the Black-headed Gull (p 102), but the flatter fore-head and longer bill of the Slender-billed Gull are good identification features. The dark ear mark is more obvious on a Black-headed Gull. In spring Slender-bills have a pink sheen on the breast. Leg and bill colour can vary from black to red.

Jan	Feb	Mar	Apr	May	Jun	Jul	Aug	Sep	Oct	Nov	Dec

Two large, white-headed gulls are found during winter along Oman's coasts. Unfortunately, they can be rather difficult to tell apart.

Heuglin's Gull

Larus heuglini
65 cm

Heuglin's Gull (formerly called Siberian Gull) is an abundant passage migrant and winter visitor to all coastal areas in Oman. In northern Oman it is probably less common than the Caspian Gull, but it outnumbers that species along the south coast.

The two large white-headed gulls are similar in size and appearance. During the winter months both are exceedingly common with flocks numbering thousands or even tens of thousands of birds. There is great variation in leg colour adding to the confusion. Field marks for the adult Heuglin's Gull include a large bill and large eyes giving the bird a mean expression, darker mantle colour, streaked neck and, often, pinkish legs.

| Jan | Feb | Mar | Apr | May | Jun | Jul | Aug | Sep | Oct | Nov | Dec |

Caspian Gull

Larus cachinnans
62 cm

Like Heuglin's Gull, the Caspian Gull is an abundant passage migrant and winter visitor, especially to coasts from Ad Duqm and northward, while it is less common along the south coast. Large flocks of these gulls often contain birds of both species.

The Caspian Gull is difficult to separate from the previous species and young birds are almost impossible to tell apart. The adult Caspian Gull has a smaller bill and smaller eyes than Heuglin's Gull and a more rounded head giving it a more gentle appearance. Other marks are less dark streaking on the hind neck in winter and often bright yellow legs. At close range a white tip to the bill may be visible.

| Jan | Feb | Mar | Apr | May | Jun | Jul | Aug | Sep | Oct | Nov | Dec |

The two species of black-headed gulls are both common winter visitors, but arrive late in autumn and leave early in spring.

Black-headed Gull   *Chroicocephalus ridibundus*
38 cm

Breeding
plumage

Winter

The Black-headed Gull is a common winter visitor with massive flocks sometimes encountered in January and February. The numbers fluctuate greatly from year to year, though. The biggest concentration is along Al Batinah coast.

While in Oman the Black-headed Gull does not have a black head. Only a few birds staying till late March and April may develop a brownish hood. In winter the head is mainly white with a small dark ear spot. In winter plumage the bird can look very similar to a Slender-billed Gull (p 99), but notice the shorter bill and steeper forehead of the Black-headed Gull. Both species may have bright red legs and reddish bills.

Jan	Feb	Mar	Apr	May	Jun	Jul	Aug	Sep	Oct	Nov	Dec

Great Black-headed Gull

Larus ichthyaetus
68 cm

Winter

Breeding plumage

A common winter visitor to sandy beaches from the northern Batinah coast south to Ad Duqm, but less common further south. Particularly common at Ras As Sawadi, Yiti, Qurayyat and the east coast from Ras Al Hadd to Ad Duqm where hundreds may be seen.

The Great Black-headed Gull is the biggest gull found in Oman. When standing next to other gulls on the beach it looks truly massive. It arrives very late in Oman and not until January is it really common. At this time the head is white with a few black spots. In February the birds change into their gorgeous breeding plumage with black head, white spots around the eyes and colourful bill. A much sought after species by visiting birders.

| Jan | Feb | Mar | Apr | May | Jun | Jul | Aug | Sep | Oct | Nov | Dec |

Terns are among the most elegant birds along the beach. Unlike gulls, most terns have the ability to dive into the sea after small fish.

Gull-billed Tern

Gelochelidon nilotica
38 cm

The Gull-billed Tern is a common passage migrant and winter visitor with a few records even during the summer months. This bird is most common on mudflats such as Khawr Jirama near Ras Al Hadd, at Sur Masirah and Barr Al Hikman and at Khawr Taqah in south Oman.

Unlike other terns, the Gull-billed Tern has a rather short, thick bill, black in colour. During autumn and winter the head is mostly white with a small black marking around the eye. In spring and summer the crown is black. This tern is often seen patrolling over the mudflats in search of insects, swooping down low over the ground and rising again. It is not nearly as common as other species of terns on the open beaches.

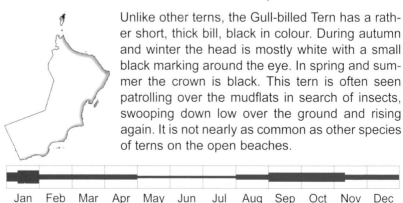

| Jan | Feb | Mar | Apr | May | Jun | Jul | Aug | Sep | Oct | Nov | Dec |

Caspian Tern

Hydroprogne caspia
52 cm

Summer

Winter

The Caspian Tern is a very common passage migrant and winter visitor with a few non-breeding birds staying over summer. Though found in smaller numbers along all coasts it is most common from Ras Al Hadd to Khawr Ghawi on the east coast.

The Caspian Tern is the world's largest tern and is larger than some of the smaller gulls. The bill is massive and bright red with a black tip making this bird stand out at the beach even in a large flock of gulls and terns. In spring and summer the head is black with much of the black retained during winter, but with numerous white speckles especially on the forehead. The call is loud, deep and rasping.

| Jan | Feb | Mar | Apr | May | Jun | Jul | Aug | Sep | Oct | Nov | Dec |

Bill colour is one of the most important field characters of terns and these two species can be separated by bill colour and size.

Swift Tern

Sterna bergii
45 cm

Winter

Summer

The Swift Tern (sometimes called the Greater Crested Tern) is a common breeding resident to a few offshore islands and an abundant passage migrant and winter visitor to all coasts around Oman. Massive flocks of several thousands have been seen on Masirah.

The Swift Tern is a large tern with a long, pointed, straw-coloured bill. In a mixed flock of terns on the beach the Swift Terns stand out by their large size. In spring and summer the head is glossy black with a crest extending onto the hind neck. In winter the forehead turns whitish, but the bill colour is unchanged throughout the year. This species may be seen on both sandy beaches and rocky coastlines.

| Jan | Feb | Mar | Apr | May | Jun | Jul | Aug | Sep | Oct | Nov | Dec |

Lesser Crested Tern

Sterna bengalensis
40 cm

The Lesser Crested Tern is an abundant passage migrant and winter visitor with many non-breeding birds staying over summer. Though sizeable flocks, mixed with other terns, have been encountered it is usually less numerous than the previous species.

The Lesser Crested Tern is quite similar to its cousin, the Swift Tern, but the Lesser Crested Tern is much smaller and has a sharply pointed, orange bill. Like its larger relative, it, too, has a black head with a crest in spring and summer, but a white forehead in winter. Normally quite easy to find in mixed flocks of terns, but you will have to scan through all birds carefully. Quite a few will then be found to have orange bills.

| Jan | Feb | Mar | Apr | | Jun | Jul | Aug | Sep | Oct | Nov | Dec |

Sandwich Tern

Sterna sandvicensis
40 cm

Spring

Winter

Yet another abundant passage migrant and winter visitor with many non-breeding birds staying over summer. Often seen in mixed flocks of terns at the water's edge on the beaches throughout Oman. Most numerous at Barr Al Hikman.

The Sandwich Tern is the same size as the Lesser Crested Tern with which it often associates. However, the Sandwich Tern has a black bill with a yellow tip. Scanning through a large flock with binoculars will most often reveal both species and probably a few others as well. Like many other terns, the leg colour is black. In flight, the Sandwich Tern looks quite pale, but the bill colour is still the best identification mark.

Jan	Feb	Mar	Apr	May	Jun	Jul	Aug	Sep	Oct	Nov	Dec

Roseate Tern

Sterna dougallii
38 cm

The Roseate Tern is a fairly common breeding summer visitor to offshore islands and may sometimes be seen along the mainland's beaches before and after the breeding season in mid-summer. Look for it at Ras As Sawadi, Qurayyat and on Masirah Island.

The best field mark for the Roseate Tern is its extraordinarily long tail extending well beyond the wing tips when the bird is standing. The bill colour is a variable mixture of black and red. Overall, this tern looks very pale and has a pinkish sheen to the breast feathers. Unfortunately, the number of breeding Roseate Terns has gone down in recent years and some colonies seem to have been abandoned altogether.

Jan	Feb	Mar	Apr	May	Jun	Jul	Aug	Sep	Oct	Nov	Dec

These two terns are easy to separate in breeding plumage in spring and summer, but during the rest of the year they look very similar.

Common Tern

Sterna hirundo
35 cm

The Common Tern is a common **passage migrant** in spring and autumn, but a less common visitor during winter and summer. Large flocks often mixed with White-cheeked Terns and with other species of terns may be found along all beaches of Oman.

Adult birds in spring are quite easy to identify on their red bill with a black tip, black cap and red legs. The tail does not extend beyond the wing tips when standing. Immature birds are very difficult to separate from immature White-cheeked Terns. With practice and patience, the white rump of the Common Tern will be a good field mark whereas the White-cheeked Tern has a grey rump in all plumages.

| Jan | Feb | Mar | Apr | May | Jun | Jul | Aug | Sep | Oct | Nov | Dec |

White-cheeked Tern

Sterna repressa
34 cm

The White-cheeked Tern is a common summer breeding visitor to off-shore islands. Massive flocks sometimes numbering tens of thousands of birds have been encountered after the breeding season, especially on Masirah Island.

In breeding plumage this bird is easy to identify on its black cap, white cheeks and sooty-grey wings and underparts. Bill colour can vary from all red to almost all black. Immature birds and birds in non-breeding plumage are much paler and are almost impossible to separate from Common Terns. The White-cheeked Tern, however, has a grey rump in all plumages, where the Common Tern has a white rump.

| Jan | Feb | Mar | Apr | May | Jun | Jul | Aug | Sep | Oct | Nov | Dec |

Bridled Tern

Onychoprion anaethetus
37 cm

The Bridled Tern is a common summer visitor breeding on offshore islands in huge numbers. Colonies may contain tens of thousands of birds. After breeding during the summer months, the birds can often be seen from the mainland, especially off southern Oman.

This tern is easy to identify with its black cap, blackish upperparts and white underparts. The white forehead and white line running over each eye has given the Bridled Tern its name. When birds fly low over a turquoise-blue sea the underparts may also look turquoise. Well after the breeding season Bridled Terns head out for the open sea to spend the winter months without setting foot on land for several months.

Jan	Feb	Mar	Apr	May	Jun	Jul	Aug	Sep	Oct	Nov	Dec

Saunders's Tern

Sternula saundersi
22 cm

Winter

Summer

Saunders's Tern is a common, but localized, breeding resident on Masirah Island and on some beaches along the southeast coast. In the loose breeding colonies individual nests are quite far apart. Outside the breeding season it is fairly common along all Oman's beaches.

This is a very small bird, not much bigger than a lark. In breeding plumage it has a triangular white mark on the forehead. The bill colour is yellow with a black tip and the outermost primaries are black as well. More white develops on the head outside the breeding season and the bill turns black. Saunders's Terns are never as numerous as most of the previous species, but wintering flocks have numbered several hundred birds.

| Jan | Feb | Mar | Apr | May | Jun | Jul | Aug | Sep | Oct | Nov | Dec |

These two birds of prey are regularly found along the coasts, but they are very different in size and in distribution.

Osprey

Pandion haliaetus
60 cm

The Osprey is a local breeding resident on coastal cliffs and offshore islands. It is also a common winter visitor and Ospreys are then easy to find in coastal areas throughout Oman. A few birds may even wander inland and can turn up at places like Al Ansab Lagoons.

The Osprey is one of the easiest birds of prey to identify. The plumage is mainly dark brown and white. The head is pale with a broad, black line through the eye. The diet consists almost exclusively of fish caught by the Osprey diving into the sea, feet first, and grabbing the fish with its talons. The legs, feet and claws are powerful - designed to hold on to the slippery prey. The fish is carried to a favourite perch to be eaten.

| Jan | Feb | Mar | Apr | May | Jun | Jul | Aug | Sep | Oct | Nov | Dec |

Sooty Falcon

Falco concolor
35 cm

Juvenile

Adults

The Sooty Falcon is a fairly common summer visitor to offshore islands in north Oman and Musandam. During their stay in Oman they can often be seen on feeding trips over the mainland at Ras As Sawadi, Seeb Airport flats, Ras Al Hamra and similar sites.

Adult Sooty Falcons are easy to recognize by their uniformly dark grey plumage, yellow bill and yellow eye ring. Immature birds have paler markings on the underside. Sooty Falcons are high speed flyers and will catch smaller birds on the wing. They are most numerous in the autumn months of August to October. By the second week in November most Sooty Falcons will have left Oman for their wintering grounds in Madagascar.

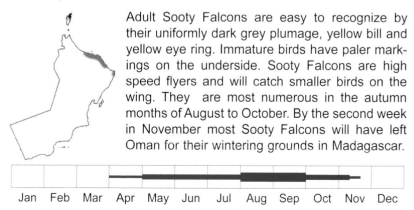

Jan   Feb   Mar   Apr   May   Jun   Jul   Aug   Sep   Oct   Nov   Dec

Most herons are dealt with under Lakes and coastal lagoons, *but this one is at home on coastal cliffs and in mangroves.*

Striated Heron

Butorides striata
44 cm

Adult

Immature

The Striated Heron is a common breeding resident along the mainland coasts and on offshore islands. Additional non-breeding birds are passage migrants. The main habitats are rocky coastlines, breakwaters in harbours and mangrove creeks throughout Oman.

This small heron is a skulker and can be quite hard to find even though it is common in the right habitats. In a mangrove creek it creeps slowly through the root system of the mangroves to emerge at the water's edge where it hunts for small fish using its powerful bill as a dagger. Adult birds are purple-grey above with a black cap and green legs. Some individuals can be very dark. Youngsters are stripy all over.

| Jan | Feb | Mar | Apr | May | Jun | Jul | Aug | Sep | Oct | Nov | Dec |

Here is the first of a long series of common waders found along the coastline and tidal mudflats of Oman.

Eurasian Oystercatcher *Haematopus ostralegus*
42 cm

The Eurasian Oystercatcher is an abundant passage migrant and winter visitor to open sandy beaches and mudflats throughout Oman. Though it is common along all beaches, Barr Al Hikman and Masirah have the highest concentrations with some 10,000 birds in winter.

This large black and white bird with a bright red bill and legs is one of the most easily recognizable birds at the beach. It is often found in small flocks feeding just at the water's edge. If disturbed they fly off calling loudly to land further down the beach and resume feeding. The plumage does not vary much from winter to summer except for thehorizontal white line on the throat that disappears in summer.

| Jan | Feb | Mar | Apr | May | Jun | Jul | Aug | Sep | Oct | Nov | Dec |

Two very common and widespread shorebirds with long, down-curved bills. The Eurasian Curlew's bill is by far the longest.

Eurasian Curlew

Numenius arquata
55 cm

The Eurasian Curlew is an abundant passage migrant and winter visitor. The largest concentration is at Barr Al Hikman where thousands winter. However, the bird is easy to find on mudflats throughout the country as well as at beaches and even on farmlands.

The Eurasian Curlew is a large wader with an extraordinarily long, down-curved bill. The species can only be confused with the Whimbrel, but the Eurasian Curlew lacks that species' striped crown and has a much longer bill. In flight, both species have a pale rump and a white wedge pointing up the back. The call of the Eurasian Curlew is a pleasant series of liquid fluty notes, lower pitched than the Whimbrel's aggressive sounding call notes.

| Jan | Feb | Mar | Apr | May | Jun | Jul | Aug | Sep | Oct | Nov | Dec |

118

Whimbrel

Numenius phaeopus
40 cm

The Whimbrel is an abundant passage migrant and winter visitor to coastal areas throughout Oman. More restricted to the coast than the Eurasian Curlew, the Whimbrel can be found on rocky shorelines, shingle beaches and coastal lagoons, but is not as numerous.

The bill of the Whimbrel is much shorter than that of the Eurasian Curlew and most of the curvature is near the tip. It is a darker bird than the Eurasian Curlew and has brown streaks on the crown. If these crown streaks are seen well, the identification has been clinched. The Whimbrel is at home on coastal cliffs, but can be difficult to spot against a dark rock. When taking off it utters a series of rapid, high-pitched calls that are quite easy to learn.

| Jan | Feb | Mar | Apr | May | Jun | Jul | Aug | Sep | Oct | Nov | Dec |

The Common and the Little Ringed Plover (p 87) can be quite hard to tell apart. Note the difference in eye and leg colours.

Common Ringed Plover

Charadrius hiaticula
19 cm

The Common Ringed Plover is an abundant passage migrant and winter visitor with a few, non-breeding birds staying over summer. This species is more coastal than its smaller relative, the Little Ringed Plover (p 87), and is rarely found away from the beaches and mudflats.

This bird is normally seen in small flocks on a sandy beach or roosting in the coastal dunes. The black eye and orange legs set it apart from the Little Ringed Plover. The short bill is red with a black tip. In flight, a conspicuous white wing bar can be seen. The Common Ringed Plover always has a complete black breast band. Plovers feed by a run-and-stop action, whereas sandpipers use a 'sewing-machine' technique.

| Jan | Feb | Mar | Apr | May | Jun | Jul | Aug | Sep | Oct | Nov | Dec |

Kentish Plover

Charadrius alexandrinus
16 cm

Male

Female
at nest

The Kentish Plover is a common breeding resident on sandy beaches and sometimes also on inland rainwater pools. In south Oman it breeds along the coastal lagoons. It is also an abundant passage migrant and winter visitor throughout the costal areas.

Unlike the Common Ringed Plover the Kentish Plover never has a complete breast band. In breeding plumage there are two sharply demarcated, black lines on either side of the breast and a black horizontal line on the forehead. Outside the spring breeding season, these bands may become more diffuse. Legs are black. It is the smallest of the plovers in Oman and can only be confused with the Lesser Sand Plover (p 122).

| Jan | Feb | Mar | Apr | May | Jun | Jul | Aug | Sep | Oct | Nov | Dec |

The two sand plovers cause much confusion and only when seen side by side is the size difference appreciable.

Lesser Sand Plover

Charadrius mongolus
20 cm

Winter

Summer

The Lesser Sand Plover is an abundant passage migrant and winter visitor along the sandy beaches and tidal mudflats. It is one of the most common birds of the coast. Huge numbers winter in the Barr Al Hikman and Masirah area where over 10,000 birds have been seen.

This species is medium in size between the Kentish Plover and the Greater Sand Plover, but size is a difficult field mark unless the different species are seen next to each other. Birds seen in late spring and early autumn have beautiful black foreheads, rufous markings on the neck and breast while winter birds lack rufous markings and have dark breast bands. Lesser Sand Plovers normally outnumber their larger relatives.

| Jan | Feb | Mar | Apr | May | Jun | Jul | Aug | Sep | Oct | Nov | Dec |

Greater Sand Plover

Charadrius leschenaultii
24 cm

Summer

Winter

Like the previous species, the Greater Sand Plover is a common passage migrant and winter visitor to beaches and tidal mudflats throughout Oman with some non-breeding birds staying throughout the year. Normally less numerous than the Lesser Sand Plover.

Great care and skills are needed for identifying the Greater Sand Plover and only with experience can identifications be certain. It is a larger bird which is noticeable when the two species occur side by side. The Greater Sand Plover has a relatively longer bill and longer legs than the Lesser Sand Plover. In late spring both species develop rufous markings on the head and the breast, but the Greater has a white forehead.

| Jan | Feb | Mar | Apr | May | Jun | Jul | Aug | Sep | Oct | Nov | Dec |

Grey Plover

Pluvialis squatarola
29 cm

Winter

Summer

The Grey Plover is an abundant passage migrant and winter visitor along the beaches and tidal mudflats throughout Oman. Large concentrations numbering several thousands are found at Barr Al Hikman and Masirah with smaller numbers elsewhere.

The Grey Plover is aptly named at least as far as its winter plumage is concerned. The bird is rather uniformly grey all over. The bill is short for a wader. An excellent identification mark is the black axillaries (armpits) seen when the bird is in flight. In late spring, just before the birds start heading north, the Grey Plover changes into its beautiful breeding plumage with completely black underparts.

| Jan | Feb | Mar | Apr | May | Jun | Jul | Aug | Sep | Oct | Nov | Dec |

Crab-plover

Dromas ardeola
38 cm

Juvenile

Adult

The Crab-plover is a common passage migrant and winter visitor, but found regularly only in a few locations such as Khawr Jirama, Barr Al Hikman, Masirah and Ad Duqm. Occasionally, a few birds are seen at Ras As Sawadi and along the south coast. Breeds on Masirah.

The Crab-plover is unmistakable with its smart black and white plumage and the massive black bill. It is one of the most sought after birds in Oman by visiting birdwatchers and is quite easy to find in the right locations. Flocks of Crab-plovers usually contain adult birds and juveniles begging for food. These young birds have a similar plumage pattern as adults but with more grey on the crown and the wings.

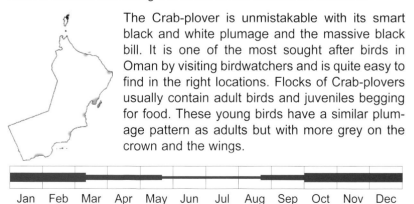

Jan   Feb   Mar   Apr   May   Jun   Jul   Aug   Sep   Oct   Nov   Dec

These two sandpipers can be tricky to tell apart in their winter plumage. In breeding plumage they are both unmistakable.

Curlew Sandpiper

Calidris ferruginea
19 cm

Winter

Summer

The Curlew Sandpiper is an abundant passage migrant and winter visitor. Autumn birds start to arrive in Oman as early as late July. They can be found along the beaches and on tidal mudflats with the largest numbers in the Barr Al Hikman area.

Late spring and early autumn birds will be in their breeding plumage and are then brick-red all over. In winter the Curlew Sandpiper closely resembles a Dunlin. Field marks to look out for include a long, down-curved bill, slightly larger and more slender body and, in flight, a white rump. Compared to the Dunlin, the bill is longer and curves in its entire length whereas the bill of the Dunlin curves mostly near the tip.

Jan Feb Mar Apr May Jun Jul Aug Sep Oct Nov Dec

Dunlin

Calidris alpina
18 cm

Summer

Winter

One of the most common and numerous waders in Oman, found along all beaches and tidal mudflats during passage and in winter. Huge flocks numbering tens of thousands of birds winter at Barr Al Hikman making this area of international importance for this species.

During the winter months the Dunlin is in its dull, greyish plumage and is not so easy to identify. Good field marks include a long bill that curves downward at the tip and greyish sides to the neck. In flight, the Dunlin shows a black line on the rump, whereas the Curlew Sandpiper has a conspicuous white rump. In late spring, Dunlins will be in smart breeding plumage with rufous spots to the upperparts and a big black spot on the belly.

Jan	Feb	Mar	Apr	May	Jun	Jul	Aug	Sep	Oct	Nov	Dec

Sanderling

Calidris alba
17 cm

Summer

Winter

The Sanderling is a very common passage migrant to all sandy beaches in Oman. Also common on tidal mudflats with the biggest concentration at Barr Al Hikman. Look for this bird in small flocks just at the water's edge on the beach.

This species is the palest of the small sandpipers in Oman. In a mixed flock they can look almost white with a black shoulder patch. Sanderlings follow each wave rolling onto the beach. As the wave comes in, the birds run as fast as their little legs will carry them up the beach. With the retreating water of the wave, the birds run back picking up food items left behind. In late spring and early autumn the birds look quite rufous.

| Jan | Feb | Mar | Apr | May | Jun | Jul | Aug | Sep | Oct | Nov | Dec |

Broad-billed Sandpiper

Limicola falcinellus
17 cm

The Broad-billed Sandpiper is a common passage migrant and winter visitor, but not nearly as common nor as numerous as the other small sandpipers on the previous pages. Good places to look for this bird include Barr Al Hikman and Khawr Ghawi on the east coast.

The Broad-billed Sandpiper is a bird of the tidal mudflats. It is rather short-legged with a black bill that curves down at the tip. Seen straight from the front the bill does indeed look broad as the bird's name suggests. An excellent field mark is a double supercilium over each eye. In fresh autumn plumage in September, the birds look very dark on the upperparts. In mid-winter, they are more uniformly grey above.

| Jan | Feb | Mar | Apr | May | Jun | Jul | Aug | Sep | Oct | Nov | Dec |

Terek Sandpiper

Xenus cinereus
23 cm

The Terek Sandpiper is an abundant passage migrant and winter visitor with many sightings of non-breeding birds through summer. Look for this bird on tidal mudflats and mangrove creeks throughout coastal Oman. Largest concentrations at Barr Al Hikman.

This interesting species can be identified both by its appearance and its habits. It is rather short-legged and has an up-turned bill. It is very active running over the mudflats, stopping suddenly looking for food and almost seems to fall on its 'nose.' The stance is rather horizontal. In flight, a white trailing edge to the wings can be seen. In most cases, the birds are seen singly, but sizeable flocks can be seen at high tide roosts.

Jan Feb Mar Apr May Jun Jul Aug Sep Oct Nov Dec

Bar-tailed Godwit

Limosa lapponica
38 cm

The Bar-tailed Godwit is yet another abundant passage migrant and winter visitor along the coasts of Oman. It can be found along the open beaches and tidal mudflats. Concentrations of 50,000 Bar-tailed Godwits have been estimated at Barr Al Hikman.

This rather large wader is easy to identify by its long legs and very long, slightly up-turned bill. In autumn and winter it is uniformly grey, but by March it changes into its brick-red breeding plumage. The tail has fine horizontal barring seen best when the bird is in flight. Bar-tailed Godwits are usually seen in flocks on the beach or on the mudflats where the birds probe deeply with their long bills in search of food.

| Jan | Feb | Mar | Apr | May | Jun | Jul | Aug | Sep | Oct | Nov | Dec |

131

Ruddy Turnstone

Arenaria interpres
23 cm

Summer

Winter

The Ruddy Turnstone is an abundant passage migrant and winter visitor along the coasts and on mudflats throughout Oman. Areas with coastal rocks exposed at low tide as well as pebble beaches are good places to look for this species. Some non-breeding birds stay over summer.

The Ruddy Turnstone got its name from the habit of using its short bill to turn over small stones looking for food items hiding underneath. It is easy to identify with its bold black and white pattern in winter, though against a dark rock it can be surprisingly hard to spot. The summer plumage includes large rufous markings, making it a very beautiful bird indeed. Ruddy Turnstones are normally found in small to medium-sized flocks.

| Jan | Feb | Mar | Apr | May | Jun | Jul | Aug | Sep | Oct | Nov | Dec |

Red-necked Phalarope

Phalaropus lobatus
18 cm

Winter

Summer

The Red-necked Phalarope is a common passage migrant and winter visitor in Oman. It is a bird of the open sea and huge flocks may be seen offshore, but occasionally, individual birds can turn up on inland pools and even in swimming pools.

Red-necked Phalaropes have a red neck only when in breeding plumage. During most of their time spent in Oman they are greyish with a black line through the eye. These delightful birds can be seen on the sea spinning round and round, picking up minute food items from the surface. They are rather tame and can often be approached quite closely. Suddenly, however, the whole flock takes off to settle a bit further away.

Jan	Feb	Mar	Apr	May	Jun	Jul	Aug	Sep	Oct	Nov	Dec

There are two species of boobies regularly found in Oman waters with the Masked Booby being more common.

Masked Booby

Sula dactylatra
85 cm

Juvenile

Adult

The Masked Booby is a common visitor off the south coast up to Ash Shuwaymiyyah, but uncommon and irregular further north. The species breeds throughout the year on the Hallaniyyat Islands. Seawatching from Mirbat and Raysut will often provide sightings of this bird.

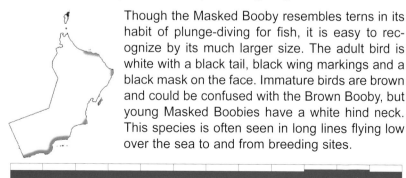

Though the Masked Booby resembles terns in its habit of plunge-diving for fish, it is easy to recognize by its much larger size. The adult bird is white with a black tail, black wing markings and a black mask on the face. Immature birds are brown and could be confused with the Brown Booby, but young Masked Boobies have a white hind neck. This species is often seen in long lines flying low over the sea to and from breeding sites.

| Jan | Feb | Mar | Apr | May | Jun | Jul | Aug | Sep | Oct | Nov | Dec |

Brown Booby

Sula leucogaster
70 cm

The Brown Booby is nowhere common in Oman, but individual birds can sometimes be seen while seawatching (watching seabirds off a rocky headland) on the south coast. Elsewhere in Oman it is very rare with a few sightings off Muscat and Ras Al Hadd.

The Brown Booby is uniformly brown on the upperparts with white lower breast and belly and a yellowish bill. Watch out for immature Masked Boobies that have a similar plumage, but with a white neck band. The brown throat of the Brown Booby reaches farther down the breast than that on the immature Masked Booby. With patience, a seawatching session off Mirbat or Maghsayl should eventually produce a Brown Booby.

Jan	Feb	Mar	Apr	May	Jun	Jul	Aug	Sep	Oct	Nov	Dec

135

Two species of cormorants are found in Oman: the Great Cormorant is the most widespread, but the Socotra Cormorant is the most numerous.

Great Cormorant

Phalacrocorax carbo
90 cm

Spring

Winter

The Great Cormorant is a large, black fish-eating bird found along rocky coastlines as well as on mudflats. In recent years large numbers have wintered at Al Ansab Lagoons near Muscat taking advantage of the many fish there.

The two species of cormorants look rather similar. The Great Cormorant is the bigger of the two and always has some bare, white or yellow skin at the chin. The breeding plumage is attained in March and consists of extensive white markings on the head and upper neck and a large white spot on the thigh. Great Cormorants are always seen in flocks, and in flight they form long, wavy lines. When sitting they often spread their wings to dry.

| Jan | Feb | Mar | Apr | May | Jun | Jul | Aug | Sep | Oct | Nov | Dec |

Socotra Cormorant

Phalacrocorax nigrogularis
80 cm

Though huge flocks of Socotra Cormorants exist in Oman waters, this species can be difficult to find. Best places to look for it include Musandam, Ad Duqm area, Masirah, Ash Shuwaymiyyah and along the south coast. It is never seen on inland lakes.

The adult Socotra Cormorant is black all over with a pale bill. It lacks the yellow throat of the larger cousin, the Great Cormorant, and do not have white markings on the head. Immature birds are brownish, often with extensive pale markings on the neck, lower breast and belly. Feeding flocks on the sea may contain 10,000 birds or more and they move forward with the rear end of the flock leapfrogging the front.

Jan	Feb	Mar	Apr	May	Jun	Jul	Aug	Sep	Oct	Nov	Dec

These two species are real seabirds. They spend most of their lives on the open sea and only come on land to breed.

Persian Shearwater

Puffinus persicus
30 cm

The Persian Shearwater is common and widespread off all the coastline of Oman from April to November. Good places from which to scan the sea include Ras As Sawadi Island, Ras Al Hadd, Masirah, Ras Madrakah, Mirbat and Al Mughsayl.

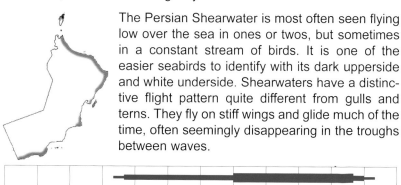

The Persian Shearwater is most often seen flying low over the sea in ones or twos, but sometimes in a constant stream of birds. It is one of the easier seabirds to identify with its dark upperside and white underside. Shearwaters have a distinctive flight pattern quite different from gulls and terns. They fly on stiff wings and glide much of the time, often seemingly disappearing in the troughs between waves.

| Jan | Feb | Mar | Apr | May | Jun | Jul | Aug | Sep | Oct | Nov | Dec |

Wilson's Storm Petrel

Oceanites oceanicus
20 cm

The Wilson's Storm Petrel is a fairly common summer visitor from Antarctica where it breeds. Look for this bird on the ferry crossing to Masirah or from the headland off the south coast, such as Ras Janjari, Mirbat, Raysut and Al Mughsayl.

This small seabird is not bigger than a swallow and is, in fact, called a sea-swallow in some languages. Its flight over the sea is fluttering and very unlike the flap-and-glide technique used by a shearwater. Though the Wilson's Storm Petrel is small it is still quite conspicuous because of its white rump. At very close range - as might be obtained from a boat trip out to sea - the yellow web between the toes has been observed.

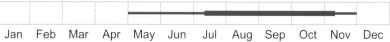

| Jan | Feb | Mar | Apr | May | Jun | Jul | Aug | Sep | Oct | Nov | Dec |

Red-billed Tropicbird

Phaethon aethereus
50 cm

This magnificent seabird is a fairly common, but rather localized summer breeding visitor to offshore islands and steep coastal cliffs. Good places to look for this species include Fahl Island near Muscat, Ras Al Khabbah and the south coast from Mirbat to Al Mughsayl.

With its black and white plumage, bright red bill and the extraordinary white tail streamers, the Red-billed Tropicbird is unmistakable if seen well. It is an excellent flyer that spends most of its time at sea coming to land only at the onset of the breeding season in April and May. Off the south coast of Oman one may see several birds, pairs and individuals, seeking out the best breeding sites during impressive aerial displays.

| Jan | Feb | Mar | Apr | May | Jun | Jul | Aug | Sep | Oct | Nov | Dec |

Swifts can be separated from swallows by their slender, curved wings. Their wing beats are rapid and shallow.

Pallid Swift

Apus pallidus
16 cm

The Pallid Swift is a common passage migrant with some birds breeding on coastal cliffs on offshore islands in north Oman and Musandam. During spring it is easy to find along the Batinah as large numbers move north. In Dhofar the status is uncertain.

Swifts are masters in the air. With their long, curved wings and aerodynamic body shape they fly at great speed as they pursue flying insects. Of several species of swifts recorded in Oman, the Pallid Swift is the most common, at least in northern Oman. From a distance it can look all black, but in good light the pale throat and sooty-grey plumage can be seen. In south Oman check out the 'Dhofar Swift' (p 245).

Jan	Feb	Mar	Apr	May	Jun	Jul	Aug	Sep	Oct	Nov	Dec

Kingfishers are colourful birds with comparatively large bills. Two species are regularly found in Oman.

Collared Kingfisher

Todirhampus chloris
24 cm

The Collared Kingfisher of the race *kalbaensis* is restricted to a few mangrove areas at Shinas and Liwa in north Oman as well as to Khawr Kalba across the border in the UAE. Recently, a few birds have been recorded at Mahawt islands near Barr Al Hikman.

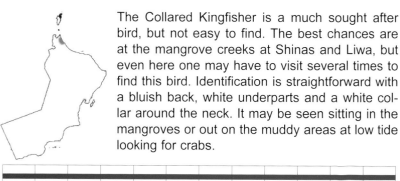

The Collared Kingfisher is a much sought after bird, but not easy to find. The best chances are at the mangrove creeks at Shinas and Liwa, but even here one may have to visit several times to find this bird. Identification is straightforward with a bluish back, white underparts and a white collar around the neck. It may be seen sitting in the mangroves or out on the muddy areas at low tide looking for crabs.

| Jan | Feb | Mar | Apr | May | Jun | Jul | Aug | Sep | Oct | Nov | Dec |

Common Kingfisher

Alcedo atthis
17 cm

The Common Kingfisher is indeed a common passage migrant and winter visitor to mangrove creeks, coastal rocks, lagoons and lakes - anywhere there are small fish to be caught. Easy to find in the mangroves at Al Qurm Natural Park near Muscat, Liwa and Shinas.

This delightful small bird is a jewel. Often one just sees a small turquoise speck zooming along a mangrove creek. If seen well it is a real beauty: massive bill, rufous underparts, turquoise and blue upperparts and white ear tufts. It can sit motionless for a long time on a branch hanging over the water. If a small fish is spotted below, the bird dives into the water and, if successful, brings the fish back to be consumed at the perch.

| Jan | Feb | Mar | Apr | May | Jun | Jul | Aug | Sep | Oct | Nov | Dec |

House Crow

Corvus splendens
42 cm

The House Crow is an abundant, breeding resident along Al Batinah coast from Khatmat Milahah on the UAE border to Muscat and beyond to Qurayyat with some birds reaching Sur. Recently, a small group has established themselves at Raysut in south Oman and is spreading from there.

This is one of the most common and conspicuous birds at fishing villages along the north coast. Dozens of birds may be seen on the beaches where fish are being cleaned. House Crows may venture up to 10 km inland in search of food especially near human habitation. Nests are large heaps of sticks built high up in trees. These birds are not always welcome as they are noisy and aggressive towards other birds.

| Jan | Mar | May | Jul | Sep | Nov |

144

Birds at lakes and coastal lagoons

The typical birds in these habitats are the large wading birds (herons, ibises, spoonbills and flamingos), a good selection of ducks and waders as well as grebes, coots and moorhens. Many of the birds from the coast, especially some species of gulls, terns and waders, will also visit coastal lagoons.

Check out the following species if a bird seen at a lake or coastal lagoon cannot be found in this section.

House Sparrow (p 24)
Laughing Dove (p 28)
Crested Lark (p 38)
Sand Martin (p 44)
Barn Swallow (p 46)
Yellow Wagtail (p 48)
Citrine Wagtail (p 49)
White Wagtail (p 51)
Desert Wheatear (p 59)
Bluethroat (p 69)
Red-wattled Lapwing (p 84)
White-tailed Lapwing (p 85)
Pacific Golden Plover (p 86)
Little Ringed Plover (p 87)
Ruff (p 89)
Cattle Egret (p 90)

Sooty Gull (p 98)
Black-headed Gull (p 102)
Caspian Tern (p 105)
Swift Tern (p 106)
Osprey (p 114)
Eurasian Curlew (p 118)
Whimbrel (p 119)
Common Ringed Plover (p 120)
Grey Plover (p 124)
Dunlin (p 127)
Great Cormorant (p 136)
Common Kingfisher (p 143)
Egyptian Vulture (p 194)
Greater Spotted Eagle (p 197)
Rock Dove (p 207)
Lichtenstein's Sandgrouse (p 222)

These two species of herons are among the most common birds seen in Oman. They are found both at lagoons and at the coast.

Grey Heron

Ardea cinerea
95 cm

The Grey Heron is an abundant passage migrant and winter visitor with many non-breeding birds staying over summer. It is at home on lakes, in coastal lagoons and even at the beach and would be hard to miss at any of these locations.

The Grey Heron is the largest of the many species of herons found in Oman. As the name suggests it is mainly grey. Adult birds have black and white markings on the head and neck while young birds are uniformly grey. This species is reported more frequently than any other bird in Oman. Basically, it can be found anywhere it can find fish, its main diet. A few birds may even turn up at inland pools.

| Jan | Feb | Mar | Apr | May | Jun | Jul | Aug | Sep | Oct | Nov | Dec |

Western Reef Heron

Egretta gularis
60 cm

The Western Reef Heron is an abundant winter visitor to coastal lagoons and open beaches throughout Oman. Some resident birds breed on offshore islands. This bird cannot be missed during the winter months in the right habitat.

The Western Reef Heron comes in two colour phases: a dark grey one that has a white throat and an almost pure white one. The latter can easily be confused with the next species, the Little Egret (p 148). The white Western Reef Heron, however, usually has a few dark feathers and has a thicker, greenish-yellow bill; Little Egrets always have black bills. Western Reef Herons fish by darting back and forth in a rather comical way.

| Jan | Feb | Mar | Apr | May | Jun | Jul | Aug | Sep | Oct | Nov | Dec |

These two white herons differ not only in size, but also in toe and bill colour - important identification features.

Little Egret

Egretta garzetta
60 cm

The Little Egret is an abundant non-breeding winter visitor with some birds found year-round. The preferred habitat is coastal lagoons and it is particularly numerous at the khawrs in Dhofar. Also common at Al Ansab Lagoons near Muscat.

The Little Egret is only about half the size of a Great White Egret. The bill is black and the legs black with greenish-yellow toes. The most similar species is the white phase of the Western Reef Heron (p 147), but that species usually has some green or yellow on the bill and legs. Little Egrets can be quite numerous with a dozen birds regularly found at Al Ansab Lagoons and at each of the Dhofar khawrs.

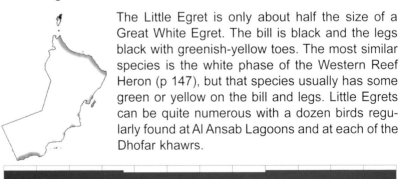

| Jan | Feb | Mar | Apr | May | Jun | Jul | Aug | Sep | Oct | Nov | Dec |

Western Great Egret

Ardea alba
95 cm

The Western Great Egret is an abundant passage migrant and winter visitor. It is common both at coastal lagoons and at tidal mudflats. Normally not as numerous as the previous species though more than 200 have been counted at Barr Al Hikman on one occasion.

With its large size (almost as large as a Grey Heron), pure white plumage, yellow bill and black legs, the Western Great Egret is easy to identify. At the lagoons it is very conspicuous even when other species of herons are present. When feeding in shallow water it is less active than the Little Egret or the Western Reef Heron. It takes a wait and see approach to fishing. In spring it develops beautiful white plumes on the back.

| Jan | Feb | Mar | Apr | May | Jun | Jul | Aug | Sep | Oct | Nov | Dec |

Though both common, these two species are not as conspicuous as the herons on the previous pages.

Black-crowned Night Heron *Nycticorax nycticorax*

60 cm

Immature

Adult

The Black-crowned Night Heron is a common passage migrant and winter visitor with some non-breeding birds seen over summer. Places to look for it include Al Ansab Lagoons near Muscat and Wadi Darbat in Dhofar. Reef-fringed lagoons are also likely habitats.

The Black-crowned Night Heron is most active at night, hence its name. Occasionally, however, a bird may be seen completely out in the open during daytime. Staying until after sunset at Al Ansab Lagoons is the easiest way to find it, though, when several birds start flying around uttering a distinctive 'quark.' Adults are beautiful black and grey with two white head streamers. Immature birds are stripy and spotted all over.

Jan	Feb	Mar	Apr	May	Jun	Jul	Aug	Sep	Oct	Nov	Dec

Purple Heron

Ardea purpurea
80 cm

The Purple Heron is an abundant passage migrant and winter visitor with a few non-breeding birds staying over summer. It is most common at lakes and lagoons with reeds that provide cover. Al Ansab Lagoons and the Dhofar khawrs are good habitats.

Despite its name, the Purple Heron is not really purple. Most birds seen in Oman are immatures that are mostly golden-brown all over. Adults have vertical stripes on the neck. This species can be difficult to spot when it hides in the reed beds. In flight the extraordinarily long and thin neck is a good field mark. Purple Herons are not numerous, though flocks of a couple of dozens birds have been seen during migration in early autumn.

| Jan | Feb | Mar | Apr | May | Jun | Jul | Aug | Sep | Oct | Nov | Dec |

These two herons are closely related and are almost impossible to tell apart in winter plumage.

Squacco Heron

Ardeola ralloides
45 cm

The Squacco Heron is a common passage migrant and winter visitor, especially to the coastal lagoons in south Oman where a few non-breeding birds stay over summer. Al Ansab Lagoons near Muscat is another good place to look for it.

In summer plumage the Squacco Heron is a beautiful bird with a golden-buff plumage and delicate white head streamers. In winter plumage it looks almost identical to the winter Indian Pond Heron being rather greyish with heavy streaking on the neck. Both species look somewhat dark and inconspicuous. However, if they take off they both suddenly look all white because of their white wings and tail.

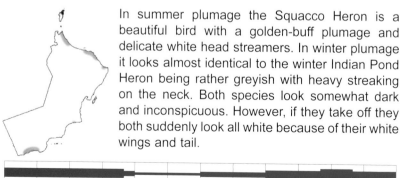

| Jan | Feb | Mar | Apr | May | Jun | Jul | Aug | Sep | Oct | Nov | Dec |

Indian Pond Heron

Ardeola grayii
45 cm

The Indian Pond Heron is a fairly common passage migrant and winter visitor, though less numerous than the previous species. It favours mudflats near mangroves such as those at Liwa, Shinas and Khawr Jirama near Ras Al Hadd as well as coastal lagoons in south Oman.

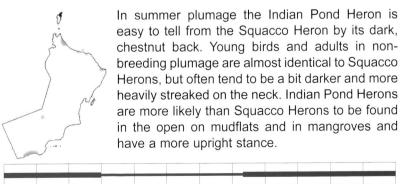

In summer plumage the Indian Pond Heron is easy to tell from the Squacco Heron by its dark, chestnut back. Young birds and adults in non-breeding plumage are almost identical to Squacco Herons, but often tend to be a bit darker and more heavily streaked on the neck. Indian Pond Herons are more likely than Squacco Herons to be found in the open on mudflats and in mangroves and have a more upright stance.

Jan	Feb	Mar	Apr	May	Jun	Jul	Aug	Sep	Oct	Nov	Dec

Two characteristic and interesting species, rather scarce in northern Oman, but very common in southern Oman.

Glossy Ibis

Plegadis falcinellus
60 cm

The Glossy Ibis is an abundant passage migrant and winter visitor to south Oman with many birds staying over summer. In north Oman it is less common, but sometimes a few birds are found at Al Qurm Natural Park, Al Ansab Lagoons and at Qurayyat.

The Glossy Ibis is unmistakable. No other large bird in Oman has a dark brown plumage and a long, down-curved bill. It is easy to find at the coastal lagoons in Dhofar with as many as 50 birds occasionally seen at Khawr Salalah Nature Reserve. The birds usually feed together in shallow water or on a wet meadow adjacent to the lagoon. They are quite shy birds and the whole flock takes off if approached too closely.

| Jan | Feb | Mar | Apr | May | Jun | Jul | Aug | Sep | Oct | Nov | Dec |

Eurasian Spoonbill

Platalea leucorodia
85 cm

The Eurasian Spoonbill is an abundant passage migrant and winter visitor. At the Dhofar khawrs some birds may be seen over summer as well. Elsewhere good numbers of spoonbills can be found throughout winter in coastal lagoons at Qurayyat, Barr Al Hikman and Ad Duqm.

With its white plumage and long, spatula-shaped bill the Eurasian Spoonbill is unmistakable. The bill colour varies with the season and with the age of the bird. Adults in spring have a large yellow spot near the tip of the bill and bare, yellow skin on the chin. In winter the bill is all black, while young birds have greyish bills. A flock of Eurasian Spoonbills feeding is fun to watch as they wade through shallow water moving their bills from side to side.

| Jan | Feb | Mar | Apr | May | Jun | Jul | Aug | Sep | Oct | Nov | Dec |

Of all the species of herons and related birds in Oman, the Little Bittern is the smallest (35 cm) and the Greater Flamingo the largest (130 cm).

Little Bittern

Ixobrychus minutus
35 cm

Adult male

Juvenile

The Little Bittern is a fairly common summer visitor to coastal lagoons with extensive reed beds in south Oman. Elsewhere, it is quite scarce though sometimes encountered at Al Ansab Lagoons and at Al Qurm Natural Park near Muscat.

The Little Bittern is a tiny heron. The adult is easy to recognize with its black crown and back that is easily seen on flying birds. Youngsters are stripy all over and rather difficult to spot as they scramble through the reeds. If frightened in the reed bed, Little Bitterns make themselves as tall as possible pointing the bill straight up. In this way they look very much like the reeds themselves. Occasionally a bird is seen out in the open.

Jan	Feb	Mar	Apr	May	Jun	Jul	Aug	Sep	Oct	Nov	Dec

Greater Flamingo

Phoenicopterus ruber
130 cm

The Greater Flamingo is an abundant winter visitor to coastal lagoons at Qurayyat, Sur, Ras Al Hadd, Barr Al Hikman, Ad Duqm and Khawr Ghawi. In southern Oman many non-breeding flamingos can be found year-round in the coastal lagoons, although elsewhere it is scarce.

The Greater Flamingo is the tallest bird in Oman and with its unusual bill and white, pink and black plumage, it cannot be confused with any other species. On the east coast the birds feed both in the lagoons and on the tidal mudflats with some 10,000 birds wintering at Barr Al Hikman and Masirah. When feeding the head is turned upside down. A flock of flamingos in flight along the coast is a beautiful sight indeed.

| Jan | Feb | Mar | Apr | May | Jun | Jul | Aug | Sep | Oct | Nov | Dec |

Grebes are waterbirds found in lakes and lagoons. They are excellent divers and can stay under water for a surprisingly long time.

Little Grebe

Tachybaptus ruficollis
25 cm

Juvenile

Adult

The Little Grebe is a small waterbird found at inland lakes and coastal lagoons. It is common only at Al Ansab Lagoons near Muscat, at Wadi Darbat in the Dhofar Mountains and at some coastal lagoons near Salalah, such as Khawr Rawri.

The Little Grebe is often heard before it is seen. Listen for the loud, drawn-out trilling song in winter and spring. Normally, it hides in dense reeds along the lakeshore, but when out in the open can be seen diving for food. Breeding is in the spring and early summer. The young chicks have black and white stripes on the head. Sometimes they ride on their parents' back with just a head sticking out from under the wings.

Jan	Feb	Mar	Apr	May	Jun	Jul	Aug	Sep	Oct	Nov	Dec

Black-necked Grebe

Podiceps nigricollis
30 cm

Winter

Summer

The Black-necked Grebe is a common passage migrant and winter visitor to lakes and coastal lagoons. Look for it at Al Ansab Lagoons, at the sewage treatment plant near Sur and in the khawrs near Salalah from Khawr Rawri in the east to Khawr Al Mughsayl in the west.

This grebe is commonly seen in open water and does not hide in the reed beds as much as the Little Grebe does. The bright red eye is conspicuous. Sometimes a little flock of birds may be seen floating together, then suddenly they all dive and disappear for a moment. Most birds will be seen in winter plumage, but in spring the birds take on a beautiful breeding plumage. A pair bred recently at the Sur Sewage Plant.

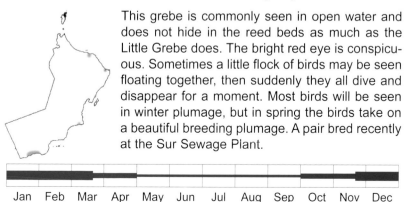

| Jan | Feb | Mar | Apr | May | Jun | Jul | Aug | Sep | Oct | Nov | Dec |

About a dozen species of ducks are common in Oman during winter, but none of them stay to breed.

Eurasian Teal

Anas crecca
36 cm

Duck
(female)

Drake
(male)

The Eurasian Teal is an abundant passage migrant and winter visitor to freshwater lakes and coastal lagoons. Good places for finding this species are Al Ansab Lagoons, Al Qurm Park, Qurayyat, Khawr Dhurf and any of the coastal lagoons in south Oman.

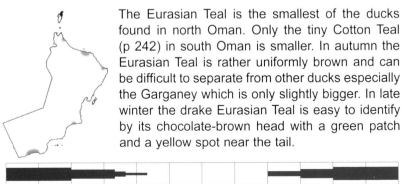

The Eurasian Teal is the smallest of the ducks found in north Oman. Only the tiny Cotton Teal (p 242) in south Oman is smaller. In autumn the Eurasian Teal is rather uniformly brown and can be difficult to separate from other ducks especially the Garganey which is only slightly bigger. In late winter the drake Eurasian Teal is easy to identify by its chocolate-brown head with a green patch and a yellow spot near the tail.

| Jan | Feb | Mar | Apr | May | Jun | Jul | Aug | Sep | Oct | Nov | Dec |

Garganey

Anas querquedula
38 cm

Female

Male

The Garganey is an abundant passage migrant and a common winter visitor. Look for this species at Al Ansab Lagoons, Al Qurm Natural Park, Khawr Dhurf, Wadi Darbat and the coastal lagoons on the south coast with the largest number reported from Khawr Rawri.

The drake Garganey in spring is one of the prettiest ducks. His broad, white line over the eye and the black-rimmed, golden feathers on the back make him easy to identify. The female and autumn male mostly brown and similar to a female Eurasian Teal though the Garganey has a black line through the eye. This can be rather hard to see and a firm identification can be tricky. In flight, large bluish wing patches are conspicuous.

Jan   Feb   Mar   Apr   May   Jun   Jul   Aug   Sep   Oct   Nov   Dec

These two species of ducks are relatively easy to identify, even the drab looking females.

Northern Pintail

Anas acuta
55 cm

Male

Female

The Northern Pintail is an abundant passage and winter visitor with large numbers found at lakes and coastal lagoons. Good concentrations can be expected in winter at Al Ansab Lagoons, Qurayyat, Khawr Dhurf and lagoons in Dhofar where up to 300 have been seen.

The Northern Pintail got its name from the long, pointed tail feathers present in both the duck and the drake. The neck is long and thin. This, with the long tail, gives the bird an elegant posture. The drake is a handsome bird with the vertical, white line on the neck and beautiful feathers on the back. The female is uniformly brown and paler than other female ducks. In flight the long neck and pointed tail are good field marks.

| Jan | Feb | Mar | Apr | May | Jun | Jul | Aug | Sep | Oct | Nov | Dec |

Northern Shoveler

Anas clypeata
50 cm

Female

Male

The Northern Shoveler is an abundant winter visitor to lakes and coastal lagoons. It is most common at Al Ansab Lagoons, Qurayyat, Khawr Dhurf and the Dhofar khawrs, especially Khawr Rawri, Salalah Nature Reserve and Khawr Al Mughsayl.

The name of the Northern Shoveler comes from its large shovel-shaped bill. Both male and female (drake and duck) have an oversized bill and the birds can be identified on the bill alone. The drake is colourful with his green head, white breast and a large rusty-coloured patch on the side and the belly. The female, like other female ducks, are plain-looking and brown. In flight, a pale blue wing patch helps with identification.

| Jan | Feb | Mar | Apr | May | Jun | Jul | Aug | Sep | Oct | Nov | Dec |

Mallard

Anas platyrhynchos
55 cm

Female

Male

The Mallard is a very common winter visitor to lakes and coastal lagoons. Favoured places are Al Ansab Lagoons, Qurayyat, Khawr Dhurf and the khawrs near Salalah. At Sun Farms in Sohar small numbers of Mallards are sometimes seen in the fields.

This familiar duck, the origin of domestic ducks, is easy to identify as far as the drake in breeding plumage is concerned. The head is iridescent green, but can look purple from a certain angle. At the rear he has smart, upturned feathers. A bright blue wing patch called the *speculum* is present in both the male and female and is bordered by black and white lines. It is particularly conspicuous when the birds are in flight.

| Jan | Feb | Mar | Apr | May | Jun | Jul | Aug | Sep | Oct | Nov | Dec |

Gadwall

Anas strepera
50 cm

Male

The Gadwall is a fairly common winter visitor, but much less numerous than the previous species. Look for it at Al Ansab Lagoons, Al Qurm Natural Park, Qurayyat, Khawr Dhurf and the khawrs in Dhofar, especially Khawr Rawri and Khawr Al Mughsayl.

Compared to other male ducks, the drake Gadwall is rather plain looking. Both male and female are basically grey in colour with a black rump. The best field mark is the white *speculum* (a patch on the wing). It can often be seen on the birds when on the water, and is conspicuous in flight. Numbers of Gadwalls seen together are never large and a flock of ten or more is unusual in Oman.

| Jan | Feb | Mar | Apr | May | Jun | Jul | Aug | Sep | Oct | Nov | Dec |

The drakes of these two species of ducks both have reddish-brown heads, but they are easy to tell apart.

Eurasian Wigeon

Anas penelope
48 cm

Males

Female

The Eurasian Wigeon is a common winter visitor to lakes and coastal lagoons. Particularly numerous at Khawr Dhurf on the southeast coast and at the lagoons in Dhofar where almost 400 have been recorded. Less numerous in northern Oman.

The drake Eurasian Wigeon is easy to recognize with its brownish head with a broad creamy stripe on the forehead and over the crown. The female is dark brown. In flight the Eurasian Wigeon shows white underparts and much white on the upper wing. Equally important for identifying these birds is the characteristic high-pitched whistle coming from a flock overhead. They arrive late in Oman and are not really common until mid-winter.

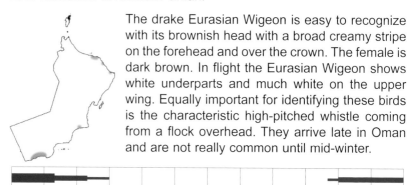

| Jan | Feb | Mar | Apr | May | Jun | Jul | Aug | Sep | Oct | Nov | Dec |

Common Pochard

Aythya ferina
46 cm

Male

The Common Pochard is a fairly common winter visitor though less numerous than the Eurasian Wigeon. Most observations are from Al Ansab Lagoons, which has a stable wintering population and from the Dhofar khawrs where 100 birds have been recorded in one flock.

The drake Common Pochard has a reddish-brown head and a pale grey back and sides. As they arrive in late autumn they will already have a splendid plumage. Females are mottled brown and grey. Previous species of ducks are all dabbling ducks. They cannot dive but are often seen up-ending with head under water searching for food. In contrast, the Common Pochard and the following two species are diving ducks.

Jan	Feb	Mar	Apr	May	Jun	Jul	Aug	Sep	Oct	Nov	Dec

These two species are diving ducks characterized by their ability to dive to the bottom of a lagoon in search of food.

Ferruginous Duck

Aythya nyroca
40 cm

Male

Though globally threatened, the Ferruginous Duck is a fairly common, but rather localized, winter visitor to Oman. Good places to look for this bird are Al Ansab Lagoons and the Dhofar khawrs, in particular Khawr Rawri where up to 40 birds have been seen together.

The drake Ferruginous Duck is rufous-brown, hence its name. It has a conspicuous white eye and the species is sometimes called the White-eyed Duck. The female is more chocolate brown. An important identification feature of both male and female is the white rump clearly visible when the birds are seen side on. Being a diving duck, the Ferruginous Duck can disappear for a considerable time under water.

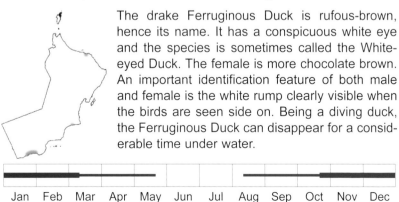

| Jan | Feb | Mar | Apr | May | Jun | Jul | Aug | Sep | Oct | Nov | Dec |

Tufted Duck

Aythya fuligula
42 cm

Male

The Tufted Duck is a fairly common winter visitor to lakes and coastal lagoons. Normally more numerous than the Ferruginous Duck, but like that species never recorded in Musandam. Largest counts have been from Khawr Rawri.

The drake Tufted Duck is a smart-looking bird. The plumage is shining black with a large white patch on the side and a bright yellow eye. He sports an elegant black tuft on the nape, hence the species' name. The white sides may be mottled grey in young males. The female is dark brown with some white around the base of the bill. She can be confused with the female Ferruginous Duck but does not have a white rump.

| Jan | Feb | Mar | Apr | May | Jun | Jul | Aug | Sep | Oct | Nov | Dec |

Common Shelduck

Tadorna tadorna
62 cm

The Common Shelduck is a fairly common, but irregular, passage migrant and winter visitor. Some years they are quite common, but in others almost absent. Most sightings are from coastal lagoons near Muscat, Salalah and Raysut.

The Common Shelduck is unmistakable. The bold black, white and rufous pattern is like no other bird found in Oman. Unlike all the other species of ducks described here, the male and female Common Shelduck look the same except that the drake has a slightly larger red knob on the bill in spring. Common Shelducks cannot dive and it is quite comical to see all the birds in a small flock up-ending at the same time.

Jan	Feb	Mar	Apr	May	Jun	Jul	Aug	Sep	Oct	Nov	Dec

Though other birds of prey may visit lakes and coastal lagoons most common is the Western Marsh Harrier.

Western Marsh Harrier

Circus aeruginosus
52 cm

Male

Female

The Western Marsh Harrier is an abundant passage migrant and winter visitor. Any lake or coastal lagoon with reed beds will have one or more Western Marsh Harriers patrolling for prey. This species is also very common on farmlands on Al Batinah and near Salalah.

The majority of Western Marsh Harriers in Oman are immature and female birds. They are chocolate brown and pale, creamy-yellow on the crown and sometimes also on the front of the wings. They can be told from other female harriers (p 92-93) by the lack of a white rump. Males are much greyer and have a distinctive wing pattern. Western Marsh Harriers fly low over reed beds or farmlands on wings held slightly up in a wide V.

| Jan | Feb | Mar | Apr | May | Jun | Jul | Aug | Sep | Oct | Nov | Dec |

Common Moorhens and Eurasian Coots are often seen together, especially on lakes and lagoons fringed by reed beds.

Common Moorhen

Gallinula chloropus
32 cm

The Common Moorhen is an abundant breeding resident, but rather local. It is very common at Al Ansab Lagoons near Muscat and at the coastal lagoons in Dhofar. They build nests hidden among the reeds. Like the Coot it has not been recorded in Musandam.

Male and female Common Moorhens are similar. With a black body and white stripe on the side, bright green legs and yellow and red bill, they are colourful indeed. Common Moorhens spend much time hidden in the reeds where croaking and splashing sounds can be heard as the birds fight for territory and chase each other. Quite often though, the birds are seen out in the open swimming with tails pointing upwards.

Jan	Feb	Mar	Apr	May	Jun	Jul	Aug	Sep	Oct	Nov	Dec

Eurasian Coot

Fulica atra
36 cm

The Eurasian Coot is an abundant winter visitor and may be found at Al Ansab Lagoons, Khawr Dhurf and the khawrs in Dhofar where concentrations of up to 200 birds have been seen. Some birds stay year round in Dhofar and breed in the coastal lagoons.

Outside the breeding season, Eurasian Coots are social birds that are most often seen in flocks. Eurasian Coots do not hide in the reeds like Common Moorhens. Black plumage with a white bill and frontal shield make it easy to identify. When swimming on a lagoon and up-ending to seek food in the shallow water, it resembles a duck, but coots - like moorhens - belong to the rail family that includes the following two species.

| Jan | Feb | Mar | Apr | May | Jun | Jul | Aug | Sep | Oct | Nov | Dec |

Like the previous two species, the Spotted and Baillon's Crakes are members of the rail family, but are quite small and secretive.

Spotted Crake

Porzana porzana
23 cm

The Spotted Crake is a fairly common passage migrant, especially in autumn, and a regular winter visitor. The best places to look for it are Al Ansab Lagoons, Al Qurm Natural Park and the reed-fringed lagoons in Dhofar. Patience will be needed, though.

The Spotted Crake resembles a small chicken. It looks similar to the Baillon's Crake, but has many spots on the wings and back and yellow undertail coverts. It is wary and seldom ventures out in the open. To see this bird one must sit patiently in the early morning or late afternoon at the edge of a lagoon where the birds forage through the mixture of mud and dead plant material. The view may be short before the bird dashes back into cover.

| Jan | Feb | Mar | Apr | May | Jun | Jul | Aug | Sep | Oct | Nov | Dec |

Baillon's Crake

Porzana pusilla
18 cm

The Baillon's Crake is a fairly common passage migrant and winter visitor. The habits and preferred habitat are similar to those of the Spotted Crake and they can be found in the same locations, sometimes even together.

The Baillon's Crake is even smaller than the Spotted Crake. Identification marks include white stripes (not spots) on the back, black and white barring on the undertail and vertical barring on the flanks. Because of their secretive nature, both species are probably more common than the number of sightings suggests. Patient observations at the edge of a reed bed may be rewarded with a quick glimpse of these alluring birds.

| Jan | Feb | Mar | Apr | May | Jun | Jul | Aug | Sep | Oct | Nov | Dec |

The two long-legged and long-billed waders presented here should not pose any identification problems.

Black-winged Stilt

Himantopus himantopus
40 cm

The Black-winged Stilt is a common, but localized breeding resident and a more widespread passage migrant and winter visitor. Look for it at Al Ansab Lagoons, Al Qurm Natural Park, Sur and Al Buraymi Sewage Plants and, in winter, at coastal lagoons in Dhofar.

The Black-winged Stilt is unmistakable with its extraordinarily long, red legs, thin straight bill and black and white plumage. It prefers shallow, freshwater pools with some cover. Al Ansab Lagoons used to be a stronghold, but numbers have declined in recent years. It is an opportunistic breeder and small numbers may breed when they find the habitat to their liking only to abandon the site a year or two later.

| Jan | Feb | Mar | Apr | May | Jun | Jul | Aug | Sep | Oct | Nov | Dec |

Pied Avocet

Recurvirostra avocetta
42 cm

The Pied Avocet is a fairly common passage migrant and winter visitor, especially on the east coast from Barr Al Hikman to Khawr Dhurf where up to 250 birds have been seen. A small flock is often present at Khawr Al Milh near Qurayyat during the winter months.

The Pied Avocet is unmistakable with its black and white plumage and long, delicate, up-curved bill. It feeds by sweeping the bill from side to side on the surface of a pond. If disturbed, the whole flock takes off, circles around a few times and settles down again further away. Like the Black-winged Stilt it is noisy and when taking off, it calls a soft, distinctive 'blyt blyt,' not as scolding as the call of the stilt.

| Jan | Feb | Mar | Apr | May | Jun | Jul | Aug | Sep | Oct | Nov | Dec |

These two small waders can be difficult to tell apart. Choice of habitat and leg colour help in identification.

Little Stint

Calidris minuta
13 cm

The Little Stint is an abundant passage migrant and winter visitor to inland lakes and coastal lagoons as well as beaches and tidal mud-flats. It is found along all of Oman's coastline with huge numbers wintering at Barr Al Hikman and other areas along the east coast.

The Little Stint can be tricky to separate from other small sandpipers, especially the equally small Temminck's Stint. They both have short, straight bills, but they can be told apart by the more mottled back pattern and the black legs of the Little Stint. On inland ponds and sewage treatment lagoons the two species are often found side by side. In late spring, the Little Stint develops numerous rufous spots on its wings and back.

| Jan | Feb | Mar | Apr | May | Jun | Jul | Aug | Sep | Oct | Nov | Dec |

Temminck's Stint

Calidris temminckii
13 cm

The Temminck's Stint is an abundant passage migrant and winter visitor to freshwater ponds, but it is not found on coastal saltwater lagoons or tidal mudflats. It is much less numerous than the Little Stint with the maximum count in one place being 45.

Superficially, the Temminck's Stint looks like the Little Stint and the two species are often found together at freshwater pools. While in Oman the Temminck's Stint has a uniformly dark back, unlike the Little Stint's more mottled appearance. The Temminck's Stint has yellowish-green legs, whereas the Little Stint has black. When taking off Temminck's Stints utter a high-pitched trill compared to Little Stints' single-noted call.

| Jan | Feb | Mar | Apr | May | Jun | Jul | Aug | Sep | Oct | Nov | Dec |

With their cryptic colouration, snipes can be difficult to spot as they tend to stay in dense cover or blend in with the surroundings.

Common Snipe

Gallinago gallinago
26 cm

The Common Snipe is an abundant passage migrant and winter visitor to freshwater habitats throughout Oman. Easy to find at Al Ansab Lagoons, Al Qurm Natural Park and coastal lagoons in Dhofar. Also common at Sun Farms, Sohar and inland sewage farms.

If seen well the Common Snipe is easy to identify. The long bill and golden stripes on the crown and back separate it from all other birds except other species of snipe. If threatened the Common Snipe may first 'freeze' and try to make itself invisible. Suddenly, however, it may take off with a loud 'reetch' call and settle under cover further away. A white trailing edge to the wings can be seen in flight.

Jan	Feb	Mar	Apr	May	Jun	Jul	Aug	Sep	Oct	Nov	Dec

Jack Snipe

Lymnocryptes minimus
18 cm

The Jack Snipe is a fairly common passage migrant and winter visitor to freshwater wetlands. In Oman, it is seen less often than the Common Snipe and can be hard to find due to its secretive habits. Al Ansab Lagoons and Al Qurm Natural Park have been reliable spots.

The Jack Snipe looks superficially like the Common Snipe, but is much smaller, with relatively shorter bill and tail, giving it a dumpy appearance. If seen at close range look for the central crown stripe that is dark brown whereas that of the Common Snipe is yellow. Jack Snipes are rather tame and will not take off until almost stepped on. Many records of Jack Snipes are of birds that were accidentally flushed.

Jan	Feb	Mar	Apr	May	Jun	Jul	Aug	Sep	Oct	Nov	Dec

The two species of redshanks look very similar in winter plumage, but in breeding plumage the Spotted Redshank is unmistakable.

Common Redshank

Tringa totanus
28 cm

The Common Redshank is one of the most common waders in Oman and found throughout the country at inland ponds and sewage farms, coastal lagoons, beaches, mangrove creeks and tidal mudflats. Tens of thousands winter at Barr Al Hikman.

The Common Redshank is a medium-sized wader with long red legs, hence its name, and a straight red bill with a black tip. It is at home anywhere there is water, fresh or salt. It is very active, looking for food in shallow water or on the mudflats. If disturbed it flies off calling loudly 'deu deu.' In flight a white trailing edge to the wings is conspicuous. Any trip to a suitable habitat between August and May should give sightings of this bird.

| Jan | Feb | Mar | Apr | May | Jun | Jul | Aug | Sep | Oct | Nov | Dec |

182

Spotted Redshank

Tringa erythropus
30 cm

Breeding

Non-breeding

The Spotted Redshank is a fairly common passage migrant and winter visitor but much less numerous than the previous species. Numbers vary greatly from year to year. It is found at inland freshwater pools but rarely in saltwater habitats.

In winter plumage the Spotted Redshank is quite similar to the Common Redshank. The bill of the Spotted Redshank is longer and thinner and is mostly black with only the inner half of the lower mandible being red. It also has a slight down curvature at the tip. In flight it does not have a white trailing edge to the wings. The flight call is a distinctive 'tjo-wheeet.' In late spring, the birds acquire an all black breeding plumage.

Jan	Feb	Mar	Apr	May	Jun	Jul	Aug	Sep	Oct	Nov	Dec

These two waders are also quite similar, but note that the Common Greenshank is larger, heavier built and has a thicker bill.

Common Greenshank

Tringa nebularia
32 cm

The Common Greenshank is an abundant passage migrant and winter visitor with some non-breeding birds staying over summer. It is found at inland pools and sewage farms as well as on beaches, mangrove creeks and tidal mudflats.

The Common Greenshank is a stocky wader, with a heavy, slightly up-turned bill and greenish legs. It is rather shy and when frightened takes off and calls noisily with a three-syllable: 'tjiu tjiu tjiu.' In flight it shows a white wedge up the back. Common Greenshanks and Common Redshanks (p 182) are found in similar habitats, but the Common Redshank is more numerous and gregarious, especially on tidal mudflats.

| Jan | Feb | Mar | Apr | May | Jun | Jul | Aug | Sep | Oct | Nov | Dec |

Marsh Sandpiper

Tringa stagnatilis
24 cm

The Marsh Sandpiper is a common passage migrant and winter visitor. Its main habitat is freshwater pools. Occasionally, it is encountered on exposed mudflats near mangroves, but is not expected on open beaches like its close relative, the Common Greenshank.

Superficially the Marsh Sandpiper looks like a Common Greenshank, but it is smaller and much more delicate. The legs are long and project far beyond the tail in flight. The bill is straight and very thin. In flight it has less white on the back and it does not have the Common Greenshank's loud, scolding call. Marsh Sandpipers are normally encountered singly or in small numbers. Flocks of more than a half a dozen birds are unusual.

| Jan | Feb | Mar | Apr | May | Jun | Jul | Aug | Sep | Oct | Nov | Dec |

The names of these two birds are rather misleading: the Wood Sandpiper is not found in woods and the Green Sandpiper is not green.

Wood Sandpiper

Tringa glareola
20 cm

The Wood Sandpiper is an abundant passage migrant and winter visitor to freshwater habitats throughout the country. Inland pools, wet farmlands and sewage farms are the main habitats. It is not found along the beaches or on tidal mudflats.

The Wood Sandpiper resembles the previously described sandpipers, but it has a shorter bill and is much more spotted on the upperside. Summer and winter plumages look similar though it is slightly duller in winter. In flight it has a white rump. It is very noisy and starts calling at any given opportunity, for example when feeding rights are being challenged by other birds, or if a birdwatcher approaches too closely.

| Jan | Feb | Mar | Apr | May | Jun | Jul | Aug | Sep | Oct | Nov | Dec |

Green Sandpiper

Tringa ochropus
23 cm

The Green Sandpiper is an abundant passage migrant and winter visitor though less numerous than the previous species. The preferred habitats are similar to those of the Wood Sandpiper: freshwater pools and sewage farms throughout the country.

The Green Sandpiper is slightly larger than the Wood Sandpiper. When the young Green Sandpipers arrive in early autumn they look almost black on the upperparts and compared to Wood Sandpipers they lack the white spots on the wings and the back. In flight the Green Sandpiper shows black underwings and a conspicuous white rump. The flight call is a characteristic, metallic 'do-eed weet weet.'

| Jan | Feb | Mar | Apr | May | Jun | Jul | Aug | Sep | Oct | Nov | Dec |

Common Sandpiper

Actitis hypoleucos
20 cm

The Common Sandpiper is an abundant passage migrant and winter visitor to freshwater lakes and pools at sewage farms. It prefers areas with some rocks or boulders, but is also seen on mangrove creeks and lawns at large hotel gardens.

The Common Sandpiper is smaller than the 'shanks' and sandpipers on the previous pages. It is rather uniformly dark and is best identified by its habits. It has a horizontal stance and often rests on rocks and boulders. While feeding it constantly bobs its tail up and down. The flight action is characteristic: a few rapid wing beats followed by a glide on wings held down. The call is a high-pitched whistle.

| Jan | Feb | Mar | Apr | May | Jun | Jul | Aug | Sep | Oct | Nov | Dec |

Black-tailed Godwit

Limosa limosa
42 cm

The Black-tailed Godwit is a common passage migrant and winter visitor to coastal lagoons in south Oman. Uncommon elsewhere though a few birds are regularly encountered on farmlands and at the coastal lagoons on the east coast.

The Black-tailed Godwit is a large wader with a very long, straight bill and long legs. While in Oman it is uniformly grey on the upperparts. Unlike its relative, the Bar-tailed Godwit (p 131), it is not found on beaches and rarely on tidal mudflats. In flight, the Black-tailed Godwit shows a prominent white wing bar and a white tail with a broad, black band at the tip. It is never numerous and flocks in Oman rarely exceed ten birds.

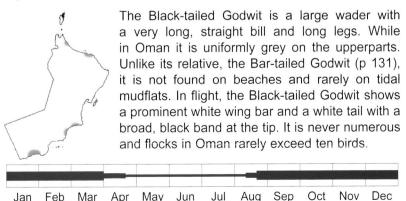

| Jan | Feb | Mar | Apr | May | Jun | Jul | Aug | Sep | Oct | Nov | Dec |

Most terns are at home on the coast, but the two terns here are marsh terns and they favour freshwater habitats.

Whiskered Tern

Chlidonias hybrida
25 cm

Breeding

Winter

The Whiskered Tern is an abundant passage migrant and winter visitor with some non-breeding birds present over summer. It can be found at freshwater lagoons, such as Al Ansab Lagoons, as well as farmlands near Sohar and Salalah.

The two marsh terns look very similar in winter and cause identification problems. The Whiskered Tern is slightly larger than its 'cousin' and has a heavier bill. The head pattern is a critical identification feature. The black eye of the Whiskered Tern is often hidden in the black mask which does not extend below the eye line. In breeding plumage from late spring the bird is very dark all over with a white chin and throat.

| Jan | Feb | Mar | Apr | May | Jun | Jul | Aug | Sep | Oct | Nov | Dec |

190

White-winged Tern

Chlidonias leucopterus
22 cm

Breeding

Winter

The White-winged Tern is a common passage migrant and winter visitor. The habitats are the same as those of the Whiskered Tern: freshwater lakes, coastal lagoons and farmlands with grassy fields in both north and south Oman.

This tern is slightly smaller and daintier than the Whiskered Tern. In winter the two species superficially look the same, but the eye of the White-winged Tern usually stands out from the black head marking which behind the eye extends to a level well below the eye. In flight it always has a white rump whereas the Whiskered Tern has a grey rump. In breeding plumage, the White-winged Tern lives up to its name.

| Jan | Feb | Mar | Apr | May | Jun | Jul | Aug | Sep | Oct | Nov | Dec |

A number of small brown birds find their home in reed beds at lakes and coastal lagoons. This one is common and easy to identify.

Clamorous Reed Warbler *Acrocephalus stentoreus*

18 cm

The Clamorous Reed Warbler is a common passage migrant and winter visitor to reed beds at lakes and coastal lagoons as well as to mangroves throughout Oman. Many birds stay year round and are suspected of breeding in these habitats.

A uniformly brown bird lacking any conspicuous features. Identification characters include a long bill and short wings with wingtips reaching only to the base of the tail on a perched bird. The best identification feature is the song, however. A continuous, croaking song may be heard from the reed beds or the mangrove. The bird stays hidden most of the time, but may come out in the open in late afternoon.

| Jan | Feb | Mar | Apr | May | Jun | Jul | Aug | Sep | Oct | Nov | Dec |

Birds of mountains and deserts

The two major mountain ranges in Oman are Al Jabal Al Akhdar that runs from Musandam to Sur and the Dhofar Mountains parallel to the south coast. Muscat lies close to the northern mountains and nearby Al Amrat Waste Disposal Site is an important part of this habitat. Typical birds of the mountains include several species of vultures and eagles, Hume's Wheatear in northern Oman and Chukar Partridge in Musandam.

Between the two great mountain ranges lies a vast desert. Most is made up of gravel plains with sand deserts in the Wahibah Sands and Ar Rub Al Khali (the Empty Quarter). The density of birds in the desert is not as high as on farmlands or at the coast, but interesting species, such as the Brown-necked Raven, Greater Hoopoe-Lark, Golden Eagle and four species of sandgrouse can be found.

Some species typical of gardens and farmlands can also be seen in the mountains and the deserts. Several are listed below.

For mountains:
White-spectacked Bulbul (p 18)
Graceful Prinia (p 20)
Purple Sunbird (p 21)
Indian Roller (p 23)
Laughing Dove (p 28)
European Bee-eater (p 34)
Pale Crag Martin (p 43)
Black Redstart (p 56)
Common Kestrel (p 95)

For deserts:
Crested Lark (p 38)
Black-crowned Sparrow-Lark (p 42)
Barn Swallow (p 46)
Isabelline Wheatear (p 58)
Desert Wheatear (p 59)
Southern Grey Shrike (p 62)
Chestnut-bellied Sandgrouse (p 67)

Two species of vultures are common in the mountains of northern Oman, but both are uncommon in the south.

Egyptian Vulture

Neophron percnopterus
62 cm

Juvenile

Adult

The Egyptian Vulture is an abundant passage migrant and winter visitor with many birds breeding and staying over summer. They are also seen on the coast scavenging for dead fish. Impossible to miss at Al Amrat near Muscat and common also at Qurayyat and Sur.

The adult Egyptian Vulture is easy to identify with its creamy-white plumage and black flight feathers. Juvenile birds are all black and immatures are somewhat mottled. In all ages, the small head and wedge-shaped tail are good field marks. Roosting flocks may contain up to 200 birds. Inexperienced birders sometimes mistake the Egyptian Vulture for an eagle because of its large size and eagle-like flight silhouette.

| Jan | Feb | Mar | Apr | May | Jun | Jul | Aug | Sep | Oct | Nov | Dec |

Lappet-faced Vulture

Torgos tracheliotus
105 cm

The Lappet-faced Vulture is a common resident in the mountains in northern Oman. A good place to find it is Al Amrat Waste Disposal Site near Muscat, though visits to Jabal Shams, the Sayq Plateau and Ibra may also provide good opportunities to see this giant of a bird.

With a wingspan of almost three meters, the Lappet-faced Vulture is the biggest bird in Oman and sightings of this bird never fail to impress. It is much bigger than the Egyptian Vulture or any of the eagles. In the morning it may be seen roosting on the hillsides at Al Amrat. As it relies on thermals to conserve energy while soaring, the Lappet-faced Vulture rarely starts flying before late morning. In flight, the short tail is noticeable.

Jan	Feb	Mar	Apr	May	Jun	Jul	Aug	Sep	Oct	Nov	Dec

Several species of eagles can be found in Oman during the winter months and Muscat has been called the 'Eagle Capital of the World.'

Steppe Eagle

Aquila nipalensis
75 cm

Juveniles

The Steppe Eagle is an abundant passage migrant and winter visitor. Large concentrations can be found at rubbish tips such as the ones at Al Amrat, Qurayyat, Thumrayt and Salalah. At times over 200 birds - of all ages - are present.

Identification of eagles can be difficult as the plumage varies with age. Juvenile eagles have not moulted any flight or tail feathers and thus look immaculate. With experience, at least four different age groups can be recognized in Steppe Eagles. Young birds which are most numerous in Oman can be identified by the pale line down the centre of the underwings and the pale, trailing edge of the wings and tail.

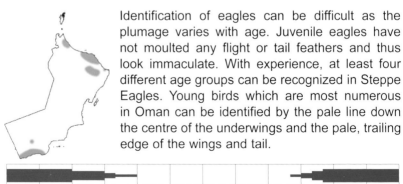

| Jan | Feb | Mar | Apr | May | Jun | Jul | Aug | Sep | Oct | Nov | Dec |

Greater Spotted Eagle

Aquila clanga
65 cm

Juveniles

Fulvescens

The Greater Spotted Eagle is an abundant passage migrant and winter visitor. Numbers are not as great as for the Steppe Eagle, but it is easy to find at Al Amrat, Al Ansab Lagoons, Sun Farms in Sohar, Qurayyat and at the coastal lagoons in Dhofar.

The majority of Greater Spotted Eagles seen in Oman are juvenile birds (less than a year old). On a perched bird the pale feather tips of the wings give a bold, spotted pattern. In flight, the leading half of the underwing is almost black and darker than the trailing half (reversed in the Steppe Eagle). A few juvenile Greater Spotted Eagles are pale on the body and are referred to as the '*fulvescens*' colour phase.

Jan	Feb	Mar	Apr	May	Jun	Jul	Aug	Sep	Oct	Nov	Dec

Eastern Imperial Eagle

Aquila heliaca
80 cm

Juveniles

Adult

The Eastern Imperial Eagle is a common passage migrant and winter visitor though less numerous than the previous two species. It is regularly found at Al Amrat, Sun Farms in Sohar, Qurayyat, in the Dhofar mountains and on the Salalah plain.

Most Eastern Imperial Eagles seen in Oman are juvenile birds. Look for a brown-coloured breast with heavy vertical streaking (actually darker underlying feathers). In flight, this streaking continues onto the underwings forming a uniform pattern of streaks from one wing to the other. Adult birds are sometimes seen, especially in southern Oman. They have a dark throat and breast and a pale nape.

| Jan | Feb | Mar | Apr | May | Jun | Jul | Aug | Sep | Oct | Nov | Dec |

Bonelli's Eagle

Aquila fasciatus
62 cm

Juvenile

Adult

The Bonelli's Eagle is a common passage migrant and winter visitor. Some birds are resident and breeding in the mountains of north and south Oman. The species is regularly found at Al Ansab Lagoons and at Tawi Atayr, Wadi Darbat and Wadi Hanna in Dhofar.

The adult Bonelli's Eagle has a pale body. The wings are dark with a pale leading edge. Immature birds are rufous. As with all birds of prey, the proportions and the shape (called the 'jizz') of the bird is important. For the Bonelli's Eagle the head is relatively small and protrudes well in front of the wings giving it a jizz resembling an oversized pigeon in flight. In Dhofar it is often harassed by Fan-tailed Ravens (p 234).

| Jan | Feb | Mar | Apr | May | Jun | Jul | Aug | Sep | Oct | Nov | Dec |

Short-toed Snake Eagle

Circaetus gallicus
65 cm

The Short-toed Snake Eagle is a common passage migrant and winter visitor to the mountains of Dhofar, less common in north Oman, but can turn up just about anywhere. Regular sightings in north Oman are from Sun Farms, Sohar and from the mountains near Qurayyat.

The Short-toed Snake Eagle has a pale body and underwings that sometimes are almost white. The head may be darker in some birds. The yellow eyes and the broad head give the bird an owl-like appearance. On the lopes of the Dhofar mountains where there is an updraft of air, such as at Ayn Hamran and Ayn Razat, Short-toed Snake Eagles can be seen hovering high in the sky on the lookout for their favourite prey, snakes.

| Jan | Feb | Mar | Apr | May | Jun | Jul | Aug | Sep | Oct | Nov | Dec |

Little Owl

Athene noctua
22 cm

The Little Owl is a widespread breeding resident in Oman. It is fairly common throughout the mountains and deserts, but due to its nocturnal habits it is not so easy to find. Look for it in Musandam and areas with rocky outcrops in the desert.

Though they are most active at night, Little Owls can sometimes be seen in late afternoon as they emerge from their daytime hiding roost. Often a pair or a small family group may be seen together. They breed in crevasses in the rocks and for nesting sites have been known even to use oil drums filled with rocks and used as markers in the desert. The call, heard at night, is a single note: 'keeah,' repeated at short intervals.

Jan   Feb   Mar   Apr   May   Jun   Jul   Aug   Sep   Oct   Nov   Dec

These two wheatears are at home in the mountains of Musandam and northern Oman.

Hume's Wheatear

Oenanthe albonigra
16 cm

The Hume's Wheatear is a common breeding resident in Musandam and the mountains of northern Oman. It can also be found down to sea level where rocks and wadis reach the coast. Look for it at Yiti and at Al Amrat Waste Disposal Site near Muscat.

The Hume's Wheatear is a smart-looking bird. Upperparts are all glossy black. The throat is black and the rest of the underparts white. The tail is like that of several other species of wheatears: a black 'T' with white sides. Sexes are alike. Easiest to find in late winter and early spring when the male sings from an exposed rock. Less likely to perch in trees than on a rock. The nest is on the ground, well hidden in a rock crevasse.

| Jan | Feb | Mar | Apr | May | Jun | Jul | Aug | Sep | Oct | Nov | Dec |

Red-tailed Wheatear

Oenanthe chrysopygia
15 cm

The Red-tailed Wheatear is a common passage migrant and winter visitor. It is most common in the mountains of Musandam and northern Oman, but may occur throughout the country where there are some rocks. Easy to find at Qurayyat and along the coast road to Sur.

While present in Oman during the winter months, the Red-tailed Wheatear is a rather nondescript bird. The plumage is mostly dark brown, but the rump and tail are rufous-brown. The preferred habitats are sparsely vegetated hillsides and isolated rocky outcrops with large boulders. Often seen perched on a rock from where it makes short foraging dashes to the ground when an insect or caterpillar is spotted.

| Jan | Feb | Mar | Apr | May | Jun | Jul | Aug | Sep | Oct | Nov | Dec |

These two species of thrushes are visitors to Oman during migration or in winter. Like their names suggest they prefer rocky habitats.

Rufous-tailed Rock Thrush

Monticola saxatilis
19 cm

Female

Male

The Rufous-tailed Rock Thrush is a fairly common passage migrant and an uncommon winter visitor. Most numerous in Musandam in April and September when dozens of birds may be present. Elsewhere it is mostly seen singly or in very small numbers.

The handsome male is unmistakable with his blue upperparts and brick-red underparts. A white patch on the back is most conspicuous in spring. The tail is red. The female is dull brown with horizontal stripes on the underparts. The tail is rather short and the Rufous-tailed Rock Thrush has an upright stance. Often seen perched on a rock, on a fencepost or on the ground where it is on the lookout for caterpillars.

Jan	Feb	Mar	Apr	May	Jun	Jul	Aug	Sep	Oct	Nov	Dec

Blue Rock Thrush

Monticola solitarius
21 cm

Female

Male

The Blue Rock Thrush is a common passage migrant and winter visitor throughout Oman. Most likely to be seen singly or in very small numbers in areas with some rocks, but may turn up anywhere, including desert oases, during migration.

The adult male Blue Rock Thrush is dark blue all over. Immature males and females are duller and more stripy on the underparts. Compared to the female Rufous-tailed Rock Thrush, the female Blue Rock Thrush is darker and less rufous-brown. In late spring the male may sometimes be heard singing from the corner of a large building. Presumably he thinks our concrete buildings resemble a rocky landscape.

| Jan | Feb | Mar | Apr | May | Jun | Jul | Aug | Sep | Oct | Nov | Dec |

Two species that are at home in the mountains and hillsides. Striolated Bunting was previously called House Bunting.

Striolated Bunting

Emberiza striolata
14 cm

The Striolated Bunting is a common breeding resident in northern Oman, but much less common in south Oman and only occasionally seen elsewhere. It is a bird of rocky hillsides, but may come to drink at Al Ansab Lagoons and may visit farmlands to feed on grass seeds.

The most obvious identification feature of the Striolated Bunting is the black and white stripes on the head. The rest of the plumage is reddish-brown with a brighter reddish patch on the shoulders. In Dhofar the Striolated Bunting can be confused with the much more common Cinnamon-breasted Bunting (p 225), but that species has an even bolder head pattern and lacks the red shoulder patches.

| Jan | Feb | Mar | Apr | May | Jun | Jul | Aug | Sep | Oct | Nov | Dec |

Rock Dove

Columba livia
33 cm

The Rock Dove is an abundant breeding resident in the mountains of north and south Oman. It may also be found at some desert oases. Large flocks may be seen foraging on the ground or coming to drink at permanent water supplies.

The Rock Dove is the ancestor of the domestic pigeon and with some individuals the two can be impossible to tell apart. A flock of domestic pigeons, however, will normally have birds of different colours, some even pure white, while in a flock of wild Rock Doves all birds look the same. Al Ansab Lagoons is a good place to look for Rock Doves and a large flock comes in regularly from the surrounding hills to drink.

| Jan | Feb | Mar | Apr | May | Jun | Jul | Aug | Sep | Oct | Nov | Dec |

These two members of the grouse family are rather shy and can be difficult to find. The Chukar Partridge is restricted to Musandam.

Chukar Partridge

Alectoris chukar
33 cm

The Chukar Partridge is a fairly common breeding resident in the mountains of Musandam. It is best found in the early morning and late afternoon in Wadi Khabb Shamsi, at As Sayh, Ar Rawdah, Jabal Harim and at Birkat Khalidiyah near Sall Ala.

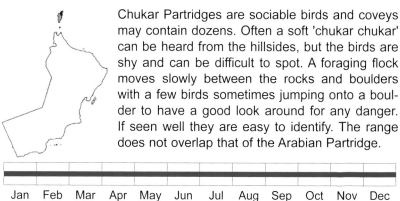

Chukar Partridges are sociable birds and coveys may contain dozens. Often a soft 'chukar chukar' can be heard from the hillsides, but the birds are shy and can be difficult to spot. A foraging flock moves slowly between the rocks and boulders with a few birds sometimes jumping onto a boulder to have a good look around for any danger. If seen well they are easy to identify. The range does not overlap that of the Arabian Partridge.

| Jan | Feb | Mar | Apr | May | Jun | Jul | Aug | Sep | Oct | Nov | Dec |

Arabian Partridge

Alectoris melanocephala
36 cm

The Arabian Partridge is endemic to the Arabian Peninsula, that is, it occurs nowhere else in the world. In Oman, it is a fairly common breeding resident in the Dhofar mountains, but uncommon in the mountains of northern Oman.

This large partridge superficially resembles the Chukar Partridge, but the two species do not overlap in distribution. In addition, the Arabian Partridge is easily identified by its broad, white supercilium. Like the Chukar Partridge, it is a shy bird and is usually encountered by chance. Likely places include the Dhofar foothills at Ayn Sahnawt and Ayn Hamran as well as Wadi Shuwaymiyyah. In winter the birds may be seen down to sea level.

Jan	Feb	Mar	Apr	May	Jun	Jul	Aug	Sep	Oct	Nov	Dec

The two species here are probably more common that the number of records show. Both are very shy and one is lucky to find them.

Sand Partridge

Ammoperdix heyi
24 cm

The Sand Partridge is a fairly common to common resident over much of Oman, but is not found among the sand dunes of the Empty Quarter, nor on Masirah. Regular sightings are from Musandam, Al Ansab Lagoons and Ras Al Jinz.

This is a small partridge that is most often encountered by chance. The male has a yellow bill and a large, white ear patch. On the flanks he has a delicate pattern of white, black and rufous stripes. The female is dull and uniformly grey. A covey of Sand Partridges moves along the hill-sides in search of seeds. The birds prefer to run away from danger and will take wing only as a last resort.

| Jan | Feb | Mar | Apr | May | Jun | Jul | Aug | Sep | Oct | Nov | Dec |

Macqueen's Bustard

Chlamydotis macqueenii
60 cm

Macqueen's Bustard (formerly called the Houbara Bustard) is an uncommon breeding resident in the central desert, particularly on Jiddat Al Harasis and in Wadi Rabkut near Thumrayt. It is also a rare passage migrant and winter visitor to other areas, mainly coastal north Oman.

Macqueen's Bustard is included in this book as it is a much sought after species by birdwatchers and because it is so important for bird conservation efforts in Oman. However, to see it, one may have to make many trips to suitable habitats in the desert. The best time of the day is early morning and late afternoon when the birds are most active. Several birdwatching tours have been rewarded by sitting quietly late afternoon in Wadi Rabkut.

Jan	Feb	Mar	Apr	May	Jun	Jul	Aug	Sep	Oct	Nov	Dec

Whereas the Desert Lark may be found in both mountains and deserts, the Hoopoe Lark is a true desert bird.

Desert Lark

Ammomanes deserti
15 cm

The Desert Lark is a common breeding resident over much of the country. It is particularly numerous in Musandam and on hillsides in northern Oman. In winter, flocks roam around and can be found at lower elevations in mountains and desert wadis.

The Desert Lark is a rather nondescript bird without conspicuous features. The best identification clue is the heavy bill with a black upper mandible and with yellow on the inner half of the lower mandible. Desert Larks are always seen on the ground where they are searching for seeds. They regularly come from the surrounding hillsides to drink in mid-morning at Al Ansab Lagoons near Muscat.

| Jan | Feb | Mar | Apr | May | Jun | Jul | Aug | Sep | Oct | Nov | Dec |

Greater Hoopoe-Lark

Alaemon alaudipes
19 cm

Display flight

The Greater Hoopoe-Lark is an abundant breeding resident in all desert areas of Oman. Often seen while driving in the desert as the bird takes off from the side of the road revealing its conspicuous black and white wing pattern. Difficult to miss on a drive from Muscat to Salalah.

This large lark is unique. The bill is long and curved and is used to dig into the ground for insects and small lizards. In early spring one may witness the unusual song flight. The bird flies up into the air, folds its wings and drops, head first, vertically down while uttering a long drawn-out whistle. Just before hitting the ground it spreads its wings and lands safely. Seeing and hearing the Greater Hoopoe-Lark is a true desert experience.

Jan	Feb	Mar	Apr	May	Jun	Jul	Aug	Sep	Oct	Nov	Dec

Asian Desert Warbler

Sylvia nana
12 cm

The Asian Desert Warbler is a common passage migrant and winter visitor. The preferred habitat is open desert with scattered bushes. Look for it along the road from Qurayyat to Sur and at the desert oases at Muntasar, Qatbit and Dawkah.

This delightful little warbler with its bright yellow eye and rufous tail is as easy to identify by its behaviour as by its plumage. The bird spends much time low in a bush or on the ground looking for insects. To be warned of any predators around it stays near a wheatear, in particular a Desert Wheatear (p 59). The wheatear sits in the top of a bush and will notice any danger. If the wheatear flies off, the Asian Desert Warbler soon follows.

| Jan | Feb | Mar | Apr | May | Jun | Jul | Aug | Sep | Oct | Nov | Dec |

Brown-necked Raven

Corvus ruficollis
50 cm

The Brown-necked Raven is an abundant breeding resident over most of Oman except in the Dhofar Mountains and the Salalah plain where it is replaced by the Fan-tailed Raven (p 234). Easy to find at Al Amrat Waste Disposal Site and at desert oases.

The Brown-necked Raven is a large bird that looks all black. Only in special light and from a certain angle can the neck feathers be seen to be dark brown rather than black. The flight silhouette is distinctive with a long, wedge-shaped tail. Outside the breeding season (late winter to early spring), Brown-necked Ravens gather in large flocks sometimes numbering a few hundred birds, especially near food or water supplies.

| Jan | Feb | Mar | Apr | May | Jun | Jul | Aug | Sep | Oct | Nov | Dec |

These two raptors are birds of the wide open desert, but neither are particularly common.

Long-legged Buzzard

Buteo rufinus
64 cm

The Long-legged Buzzard is a fairly common passage migrant and winter visitor and may turn up almost anywhere. A few birds are breeding residents in the central desert. Look for this species at Muntasar, Al Balid Farm and, during winter, in the Dhofar Mountains.

The Long-legged Buzzard is a pale raptor with a reddish tail. It is smaller and has a less powerful bill than an eagle. In flight, an additional identification feature is a black spot and 'comma' at the carpal point (the wrist located halfway out the leading edge of the wing). At Muntasar and Dawkah up to 30 birds have been seen gathering to drink during the hot season, but normally, sightings are of single birds.

| Jan | Feb | Mar | Apr | May | Jun | Jul | Aug | Sep | Oct | Nov | Dec |

Golden Eagle

Aquila chrysaetos
78 cm

The Golden Eagle is a fairly common breeding resident, but restricted to the central desert region of Oman. The most reliable place to see this bird is at Muntasar where, especially in the hot season, several Golden Eagles may come to drink.

This is a powerful and majestic eagle. The name arises from the golden feathers on the back of the neck of the adult bird. The rest of the body and the wings are dark brown. Immature birds have a large, white patch on the wings and at the base of the tail. As the eagle grows older and attains adulthood (after six or seven years), these white patches gradually disappear. As with most birds of prey, the female is the larger.

Jan	Feb	Mar	Apr	May	Jun	Jul	Aug	Sep	Oct	Nov	Dec

217

These two, rather large, waders are true desert birds and have adapted to a life in arid surroundings.

Spotted Thick-knee

Burhinus capensis
38 cm

The Spotted Thick-knee is a fairly common breeding resident in the central desert and south Oman. Look for it on the Jiddat Al Harasis, in Wadi Gharm near Ras Madrakah and on the farmlands and golf courses in and around Salalah.

The name of this bird refers to the thick joint on its legs. As birds walk on their toes this joint is actually the heel while the knee is hidden in the belly feathers. The cryptic colouration of the Spotted Thick-knee helps it blend in with its desert surroundings and the bird can be difficult to spot. Moreover, as suggested by the large eyes, the bird is most active at night when, during courtship, Whimbrel-like flight calls may be heard.

Jan	Feb	Mar	Apr	May	Jun	Jul	Aug	Sep	Oct	Nov	Dec

Cream-coloured Courser

Cursorius cursor
26 cm

The Cream-coloured Courser is a common passage migrant and winter visitor to deserts and arid farmlands. A few birds nest in the central part of Oman. Look for it on farmlands in the desert and near Sohar and Salalah as well as on the Jiddat Al Harasis.

Except for the beautifully bold head pattern, this species with its uniformly beige colour blends in perfectly with its arid surroundings. If the bird stands still it can be difficult to see. The black and white stripes through and above each eye meet at the back of the neck. When looking for food or escaping danger, the bird prefers to run. Only as a last resort will it take wing. In flight the outer half of each wing is black.

Jan	Feb	Mar	Apr	May	Jun	Jul	Aug	Sep	Oct	Nov	Dec

Sandgrouse are birds of deserts and arid landscapes. These two species in particular are birds of the central deserts in Oman.

Crowned Sandgrouse

Pterocles coronatus
28 cm

Male

The Crowned Sandgrouse is a common breeding resident of flat, stony plains in central and southern Oman. Good places to look for it are Jaluni, Muntasar, Qatbit and Dawkah where the birds come to drink, early to mid-morning, often in large flocks.

The male Crowned Sandgrouse is easy to identify based on the black, vertical lines on either side of the bill. The rest of the body is sandy grey and brown with pale spots on the wing. The female is similar, but lacks the male's bold head pattern. At permanent water holes in the desert the birds arrive in large flocks and while in flight give a characteristic, four to five syllable call that sounds like 'ge-bäcked po-ta-to.'

| Jan | Feb | Mar | Apr | May | Jun | Jul | Aug | Sep | Oct | Nov | Dec |

Spotted Sandgrouse

Pterocles senegallus
30 cm

Male

The Spotted Sandgrouse is a fairly common breeding resident in sandy deserts in central and southern Oman. Hundreds or even thousands may come to drink early to mid-morning at Muntasar and Qatbit where they easily outnumber the previous species.

The female Spotted Sandgrouse is profusely spotted all over while the male is more uniformly coloured. Huge flocks fly to permanent water holes in the desert. In flight they give a two-syllable call: 'qa-ta qa-ta', or 'wi-dow wi-dow' that can easily be told from the call of the Crowned Sandgrouse. Like all sandgrouse, the male soaks up water in his belly feathers and returns with it to waiting chicks many kilometers away.

Jan	Feb	Mar	Apr	May	Jun	Jul	Aug	Sep	Oct	Nov	Dec

Lichtenstein's Sandgrouse *Pterocles lichtensteinii*
27 cm

Female

Male

The Lichtenstein's Sandgrouse is a fairly common and widespread breeding resident over most of Oman, but absent from Masirah and the Empty Quarter. More difficult to see than other sandgrouse as it comes to drink after dark, for example at Al Ansab Lagoons.

This is perhaps the most beautiful of the sandgrouse found in Oman. In the fading light of the day one may be able to see these birds in the headlights coming to drink. During daytime one may come across single, feeding birds or pairs. The male is particularly handsome with his broad black and white stripes on the breast and narrow horizontal barring over most of the upperparts. The female is barred all over.

| Jan | Feb | Mar | Apr | May | Jun | Jul | Aug | Sep | Oct | Nov | Dec |

Birds of Dhofar

A number of common birds are found in Dhofar, but do not occur or are very rare in the rest of Oman. These birds are mainly African in origin and the species find their northernmost distribution in Dhofar. Most of the birds presented in the previous sections are also found in Dhofar, but the birds in this section are Dhofar specialities. The presence of these birds creates a striking difference between birdlife in Dhofar and the rest of Oman.

From a birdwatching point of view, the short trip by plane from Muscat to Salalah might seem like traveling to a different continent - yet one has not even left the country.

The reason for this diversity is the different climate in Dhofar, with its summer monsoon and therefore different plants and trees. Natural boundaries, such as oceans and deserts, separate bird populations and some species cannot cross the 800 km of arid land between north and south Oman.

This adds to the excitement of birdwatching in Oman. Whereas the north sees a mixture of birds from Europe and Asia, the birds of Dhofar are closely related to African species. Thus within the borders of Oman, there are common birds from three continents. In zoo-geographical terms, the birds in north Oman are from the West Palearctic and the Oriental regions, while many birds in Dhofar are from the Afrotropical region. More than any other country in the world, the Sultanate of Oman lies at the crossroads of avian biodiversity.

These two birds are exceedingly common in Dhofar; yet they have never been observed north of the Dhofar mountains.

Rüppell's Weaver

Ploceus galbula
15 cm

Female

Male at nest

The Rüppell's Weaver is an abundant breeding resident in south Oman. The main habitats include gardens, parks and wadis in the foothills. It is related to the House Sparrow (p 24) of northern Oman, but the two species do not meet in Oman.

The male Rüppell's Weaver is unmistakable from February to June in his bright yellow and black appearance. The rest of the year he resembles the female, a rather uniformly grey to olive-green bird. The calls include nasal squeaks that are easy to learn. In spring, the male builds several beautiful hanging nests with the entrance hole at the bottom. An interested female inspects the nests and chooses the strongest one.

| Jan | Feb | Mar | Apr | May | Jun | Jul | Aug | Sep | Oct | Nov | Dec |

Cinnamon-breasted Bunting

Emberiza tahapisi
17 cm

The Cinnamon-breasted Bunting (formerly called the African Rock Bunting) is an abundant breeding resident in the mountains and foothills in Dhofar. Outside the summer monsoon it is often the most common bird at Ayn Razat, Ayn Hamran and Ayn Sahnawt.

The male is a striking bird with his bold, black and white head pattern and rusty colours on its breast and belly. Females and immature birds are similar, but more subdued in colour. They resemble the Striolated Bunting (p 206), but lack that species' rufous shoulder patch and are much more common. Cinnamon-breasted Buntings gather in good numbers to drink wherever there is fresh water during the dry season.

| Jan | Feb | Mar | Apr | May | Jun | Jul | Aug | Sep | Oct | Nov | Dec |

These small birds are common wherever there are trees and bushes in the Salalah area and the Dhofar hills.

Abyssinian White-eye

Zosterops abyssinicus

12 cm

The Abyssinian White-eye (formerly called the White-breasted White-eye) is an abundant breeding resident in garden areas, parks and woodlands in south Oman. A few birds may occasionally wander further north and some have reached Qatbit. Easy to find near the *ayns*.

The conspicuous, white ring of feathers around the eye has given the name to this family. The Abyssinian White-eye is an active bird moving through the leaves on a tree and is often hanging upside down looking for insects and larvae. It blends in well with the foliage and can be difficult to get a good look at, as it constantly moves around. The call is a soft, drawn-out whistle that can aid in identification.

Jan	Feb	Mar	Apr	May	Jun	Jul	Aug	Sep	Oct	Nov	Dec

African Silverbill

Lonchura cantans
11 cm

The African Silverbill is a common breeding resident in south Oman. Easy to find on farmlands, in parks and gardens, and in the foothills, anywhere there are grass seeds to be found. The birds are social and always seen in small to large flocks.

Like the Indian Silverbill (p 25) of northern Oman, the African Silverbill has a large, silvery-grey bill. The two species do not overlap in distribution. They could easily be told apart, though, by the colour of the rump: white in the Indian Silverbill, black or dark brown in the African Silverbill. When they are not feeding, these birds spend much time preening each other, which they seem to enjoy thoroughly.

| Jan | Feb | Mar | Apr | May | Jun | Jul | Aug | Sep | Oct | Nov | Dec |

Two species of sunbirds are common in south Oman. They resemble the Purple Sunbird (p 21) that is abundant in northern Oman.

Shining Sunbird

Cinnyris habessinicus
13 cm

Female

Male

The Shining Sunbird is a common breeding resident in parks and gardens in south Oman. Easy to find at Ayn Razat and Ayn Hamran, and when there are flowering trees and plants, dozens of birds may be present.

The Shining Sunbird is the largest of the sunbirds in Oman. The male is glossy black with a broad red breast band. The female is dark grey and resembles the female Palestine Sunbird but is larger and has a longer, more curved bill. The call of the Shining Sunbird is a loud trill that is helpful in locating and identifying the bird. It feeds on the nectar of flowers, but will also take insects, at least when feeding young in the nest.

Jan	Feb	Mar	Apr	May	Jun	Jul	Aug	Sep	Oct	Nov	Dec

Palestine Sunbird

Cinnyris osea
11 cm

Female

Male

The Palestine Sunbird is a common breeding resident in south Oman, but less numerous than the previous species. The habitats include parks, gardens and dry hillsides. Ayn Razat, Ayn Hamran and Tawi Atayr are good places to locate this species.

The habits of the Palestine Sunbird are similar to those of the Shining Sunbird. The birds move from flower to flower to lick up nectar with their sticky tongues. Flowering *Acacia* trees and Sodum's Apple are favourite food plants. The male Palestine Sunbird lacks the red breast band of the Shining Sunbird, is smaller and has a shorter bill. The females look similar, but the size difference is obvious if they are seen together.

| Jan | Feb | Mar | Apr | May | Jun | Jul | Aug | Sep | Oct | Nov | Dec |

Two more African species with distributions just reaching Dhofar. The pigeon is partly migratory while the flycatcher is resident.

Bruce's Green Pigeon

Treron waalia
31 cm

Bruce's Green Pigeon is a fairly common breeding summer visitor to foothills and parks in Dhofar. Some birds stay over winter. Look for them where there are big fig trees with ripe fruit, such as at Ayn Razat, Ayn Hamran, Wadi Darbat and Wadi Hanna.

This beautiful pigeon is greenish-grey above and has a bright yellow belly. Seeing the bird is a different matter, though, as it blends in extremely well with the green foliage in the top of the fig trees. The call is a drawn out 'wheeo' and various chattering, completely different from the call of other doves and pigeons in Oman. When taking off the wing tips make loud clapping noises when they slap together.

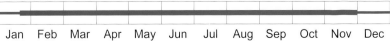

| Jan | Feb | Mar | Apr | May | Jun | Jul | Aug | Sep | Oct | Nov | Dec |

African Paradise Flycatcher

Terpsiphone viridis
20 cm (adult male: 36 cm)

The African Paradise Flycatcher is a common breeding resident in any wooded area in Dhofar. In the dry season, they are particularly numerous near fresh water, such as at Ayn Razat, Ayn Hamran, Wadi Darbat and Wadi Hanna.

The adult male African Paradise Flycatcher in breeding plumage is exceptionally beautiful with his white wing patches and white tail streamers that are longer than the body. Females and young males are more numerous. All can be recognized by their bluish-black head, red back and red tail. This species spends most of the time in the shade of trees, especially if the weather is hot. From its perch it makes short flights to catch insects.

| Jan | Feb | Mar | Apr | May | Jun | Jul | Aug | Sep | Oct | Nov | Dec |

These two members of the thrush family are most common in the Dhofar Mountains, but their ranges also extend north into the desert.

Blackstart

Cercomela melanura
15 cm

The Blackstart is a common breeding resident in the mountains and foothills of south Oman with the range extending northward to at least Thumrayt. Easy to find in the drier areas of Ayn Razat, Ayn Hamran and Tawi Atayr.

The name of the Blackstart refers to its black tail, the rest of the bird is uniformly dark grey. It sits on a branch quietly looking for insects in the air or on the ground below. The preferred habitats are arid plains and dry hillsides with scattered trees and bushes. It does not come to freshwater pools. Normally seen singly, though several Blackstarts may be seen scattered throughout a suitable habitat.

| Jan | Feb | Mar | Apr | May | Jun | Jul | Aug | Sep | Oct | Nov | Dec |

Arabian Wheatear

Oenanthe lugentoides
14 cm

Male

Female

The Arabian Wheatear is a common breeding resident in the Dhofar mountains with the range extending northeast-ward through Wadi Shuwaymiyyah and Sawqirah to the Huqf Escarpment west of Ad Duqm. Also present on Al Hallaniyyat Islands.

The male Arabian Wheatear resembles several other black and white wheatears in Oman, but can be recognized by his black plumage with white crown, belly and rump and yellowish undertail coverts. The female is uniformly greyish-brown. This wheatear is a bird of dry hillsides and mountains with scattered rocks and boulders. Only on the Hallaniyyat Islands can it be found down to sea level.

| Jan | Feb | Mar | Apr | May | Jun | Jul | Aug | Sep | Oct | Nov | Dec |

These two black birds are typical of the Dhofar Mountains and foothills. They are most often seen in flocks flying along the hillsides.

Fan-tailed Raven

Corvus rhipidurus
47 cm

The Fan-tailed Raven is an abundant breeding resident in the Dhofar Mountains where it replaces the Brown-necked Raven (p 215) found in the rest of Oman. Any trip along the mountain roads in Dhofar should produce sightings of Fan-tailed Ravens.

This all-black bird is smaller than the Brown-necked Raven and has a different flight silhouette. The wings are broader and the tail shorter and often fanned, hence the name. The Fan-tailed Ravens are most common in the mountains and foothills where they chase each other and harass any large bird of prey or just tumble in the uprising air currents. They also come to coastal cliffs and villages.

Jan   Feb   Mar   Apr   May   Jun   Jul   Aug   Sep   Oct   Nov   Dec

Tristram's Starling

Onychognathus tristramii
25 cm

The Tristram's Starling is an abundant breeding resident in Dhofar. Impossible to miss in the mountains, especially near farms, at Tawi Atayr and in coastal villages such as Rakhyut and Taqah where, in winter, hundreds may be present.

The Tristram's Starling is a large, almost all black starling. The male is glossy black, the female sooty black. Both have rufous flight feathers seen as a thin line on the folded wing of a perched bird, but very conspicuous when the birds are in flight. They are noisy and frequently give out a pleasing, drawn out whistle 'wheeo.' Sometimes seen perched on a camel looking for parasites in the skin.

Jan	Feb	Mar	Apr	May	Jun	Jul	Aug	Sep	Oct	Nov	Dec

These two, rather nondescript, birds are not difficult to find in appropriate habitats.

Singing Bush Lark

Mirafra cantillans
13 cm

The Singing Bush Lark is a common migrant breeder to farmlands near Salalah and areas with grassy plains in the Dhofar hills. Impossible to miss at Jarziz Farm and Sahnawt Farm in April and May when hundreds or even thousands may be present.

A few birds may be heard singing on the farms already in late January. From April, however, the sky over the grassy fields is filled with these delightful songsters. Each bird hangs in the air and lets out his jubilant song that may last 10 minutes or more before he swoops down onto the grass only to continue his advertising a few minutes later. Occasionally, he may perch on the water pivots and sing from there.

| Jan | Feb | Mar | Apr | May | Jun | Jul | Aug | Sep | Oct | Nov | Dec |

Yemen Serin

Crithagra menachensis
12 cm

The Yemen Serin is a highly localised breeding resident in the huge sink hole at Tawi Atayr in the Dhofar Mountains. This species has only recently been discovered when a team of cave explorers found it breeding deep inside the hole. A few birds have been seen elsewhere.

A telescope may be needed to see the Yemen Serin inside the sink hole. A walk around the edge of the hole, especially along the north side, however, should produce sightings of several birds as they come up to feed on the surrounding hillsides. The bird has the thick bill of a seedeater and is uniformly grey without any obvious markings. This is a much sought after species for visiting as well as resident birdwatchers.

Jan	Feb	Mar	Apr	May	Jun	Jul	Aug	Sep	Oct	Nov	Dec

These two species are typical African birds that migrate north in spring to breed in southwest Arabia, including Dhofar.

Dideric Cuckoo

Chrysococcyx caprius
18 cm

The Dideric Cuckoo is a fairly common summer breeding visitor to the foothills of the Dhofar Mountains. It is more often heard than seen, but good places to look for it include Ayn Razat, Ayn Hamran and Wadi Darbat.

In early summer the calls of the Dideric Cuckoo can be heard from the hillsides: 'dee-dee-dee-de-ric,' repeated endlessly. The bird can be difficult to spot in the green foliage, but when seen well, it is unmistakable. Like other cuckoos it does not build a nest of its own. The female sneaks into several nests of Rüppell's Weavers (p 224) and lays a single egg in each nest, much to the annoyance of the owners.

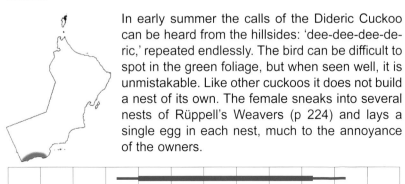

| Jan | Feb | Mar | Apr | May | Jun | Jul | Aug | Sep | Oct | Nov | Dec |

Grey-headed Kingfisher

Halcyon leucocephala
20 cm

The Grey-headed Kingfisher is a common summer breeding visitor to the foothills of the Dhofar Mountains. Easy to find in most wooded areas such as Ayn Razat, Ayn Hamran, Wadi Darbat and Wadi Hanna. In autumn, it can also be seen on farmlands.

This is one of the most brilliantly coloured birds in Oman: aquamarine wings and tail, deep rufous belly and bright red bill and feet. Often perches on a twig right out in the open looking for prey on the ground below. Unlike the other two kingfishers in Oman, the Common (p 143) and the Collared Kingfisher (p 142), the Grey-headed Kingfisher is not associated with water. The call is a loud, far-reaching clatter.

Jan	Feb	Mar	Apr	May	Jun	Jul	Aug	Sep	Oct	Nov	Dec

In Oman, these two birds of prey breed only in Dhofar, and they can be difficult to find.

Black Kite

Milvus migrans
55 cm

The Black Kite is a localised breeding resident in Dhofar, and though not common, may be found near coastal villages with tall coconut palms that are used for nest building. It is also an uncommon passage migrant and winter visitor to the rest of the country.

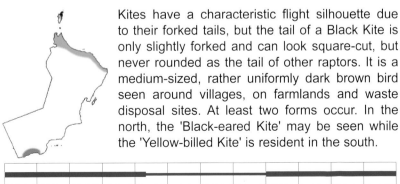

Kites have a characteristic flight silhouette due to their forked tails, but the tail of a Black Kite is only slightly forked and can look square-cut, but never rounded as the tail of other raptors. It is a medium-sized, rather uniformly dark brown bird seen around villages, on farmlands and waste disposal sites. At least two forms occur. In the north, the 'Black-eared Kite' may be seen while the 'Yellow-billed Kite' is resident in the south.

Jan	Feb	Mar	Apr	May	Jun	Jul	Aug	Sep	Oct	Nov	Dec

Verreaux's Eagle

Aquila verreauxii
90 cm

The Verreaux's Eagle is an uncommon breeding resident in the Dhofar Mountains and is included in this book because it is a magnificent and much sought after bird. Look for it in the hills above Ayn Hamran, in Wadi Darbat and the wadi behind Khawr Al Mughsayl.

The adult bird is all black except for large, white patches on the wing, a white rump and a white line running up each side of the back. The flight silhouette is characteristic with a strongly curved, trailing edge to the wing giving the appearance of a narrow base to the wing. The immatures are mottled grey and brown, but with the same flight silhouette. Patiently scanning the sky at the upper end of Ayn Hamran may produce a sighting.

Jan	Feb	Mar	Apr	May	Jun	Jul	Aug	Sep	Oct	Nov	Dec

Curiously, a few birds of these two species, both of Indian origin, arrive in the autumn at the coastal lagoons in Dhofar.

Cotton Pygmy Goose   *Nettapus coromandelianus*
33 cm

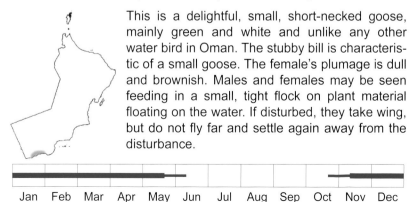

The Cotton Pygmy Goose is a fairly common winter visitor to the khawrs in Dhofar, especially Khawr Sawli, Khawr Rawri, East Khawr, Khawr Al Mughsayl and Khawr Salalah Nature Reserve. They arrive late in autumn, but stay well into May before heading back east.

This is a delightful, small, short-necked goose, mainly green and white and unlike any other water bird in Oman. The stubby bill is characteristic of a small goose. The female's plumage is dull and brownish. Males and females may be seen feeding in a small, tight flock on plant material floating on the water. If disturbed, they take wing, but do not fly far and settle again away from the disturbance.

Jan	Feb	Mar	Apr	May	Jun	Jul	Aug	Sep	Oct	Nov	Dec

Pheasant-tailed Jacana   *Hydrophasianus chirurgus*
31 cm (48 cm when breeding)

Winter

Summer

The Pheasant-tailed Jacana is a fairly common winter visitor to Wadi Darbat and coastal lagoons in Dhofar. Occasionally, a few birds stay over summer and may even breed. Easy to find at Khawr Rawri, Khawr Taqah and Khawr Al Mughsayl. Numbers have declined in recent years.

Few birds look so different in winter and summer plumage. While in Oman the Pheasant-tailed Jacana is a brownish bird with a white throat, a golden nape and a black line on the side of the neck. In breeding plumage from late May it is transformed into a mainly black bird with an extraordinarily long black tail. The wings - summer or winter - are white. With its long toes it can walk on floating plant material in search of food.

| Jan | Feb | Mar | Apr | May | Jun | Jul | Aug | Sep | Oct | Nov | Dec |

These two species are unusual, but for different reasons: one is a skulker and difficult to see, the other is clouded in mystery!

Black-crowned Tchagra

Tchagra senegalus
22 cm

The Black-crowned Tchagra is a fairly common breeding resident in the Dhofar Mountains and foothills. Patience may be needed to see it, but good places to look for it include drier areas of Ayn Hamran and Ayn Sahnawt.

If seen well this bird is unmistakable with its bold head pattern and long tail ending in a white tip. It spends most of its time well hidden in the undergrowth pecking through the leaf litter in search of food. But be patient and the bird may eventually come out in the open, jump onto a branch or hop to the next potential feeding site. It is seldom seen high in a tree or in flight, preferring instead to stay low and out of sight.

Jan	Feb	Mar	Apr	May	Jun	Jul	Aug	Sep	Oct	Nov	Dec

'Dhofar Swift'

Apus sp.
16 cm

This species is a mystery. From April or May large numbers of swifts gather at the coastal cliffs in Dhofar and spend the summer there. It is easy to find at Khawr Rawri and the cliffs east and west of there. Feeding parties may also be seen over the farmlands and foothills.

These swifts look somewhat like the Pallid Swift (p 141), but seem more scaly on the underside. Many observers now believe they are Forbes-Watson's Swift *Apus berliozi*, but others have considered an eatern race of Common Swift *Apus apus pekinensis*. Detailed scientific studies involving DNA analysis will probably be needed to sort out the problem. Until then, we can enjoy their acrobatic flights and simply refer to them as 'Dhofar Swifts.'

| Jan | Feb | Mar | Apr | May | Jun | Jul | Aug | Sep | Oct | Nov | Dec |

Additional species

When birdwatching in Oman the great majority of species seen should be found in this book. Eventually, however, you may come across a bird that just does not seem to fit anything in the book. This is possible, of course, as we have presented only 225 species of a total of 498 species recorded in Oman. On these two pages we include an additional 25 species that may occasionally be seen. The same colour coding for habitats as in the rest of the book has been used.

Richard's Pipit, 18 cm
Anthus richardi

Long-billed Pipit, 17 cm
Anthus similis

Common Nightingale, 16 cm
Luscinia megarhynchos

Northern Wheatear, 15 cm
Oenanthe oenanthe

Pied Wheatear, 15 cm
Oenanthe pleschanka

Hooded Wheatear, 17 cm
Oenanthe monacha

Black-throated Thrush, 23 cm
Turdus atrogularis

Song Thrush, 22 cm
Turdus philomelos

Corn Bunting, 17 cm
Emberiza calandra

Upcher's Warbler, 15 cm
Hippolais languida

Ménétriés's Warbler, 13 cm
Sylvia mystacea

Arabian Warbler, 14 cm
Sylvia leucomelaena

Pale Rockfinch, 14 cm
Carpospiza brachydactyla

Yellow-throated Sparrow, 13 cm
Gymnoris xanthocollis

Spanish Sparrow, 15 cm
Passer hispaniolensis

Eurasian Scops Owl, 19 cm
Otus scops

Barn Owl, 24 cm
Tyto alba

Trumpeter Finch, 14 cm
Bucanetes githagineus

Red-backed Shrike, 18 cm
Lanius collurio

Booted Eagle, 50 cm
Aquila pennata

Eurasian Hobby, 34 cm
Falco subbuteo

Small Pratincole, 17 cm
Glareola lactea

Abdim's Stork, 80 cm
Ciconia abdimii

Great Knot, 27 cm
Calidris tenuirostris

Yellow Bittern, 34 cm
Ixobrychus sinensis

Index of scientific names

Index and checklist of the birds of Oman

This list presents in alphabetic order all the 498 species of birds accepted by the Oman Bird Records Committee. Species included in this guide are in **bold** and the page number is given. Against each species are two small check boxes. Use them to tick off a species when you have seen it and thus keep a running total of the number of birds you have recorded. Two people can use the list with one column of boxes used by each person. A friendly competition can emerge.

☐☐ **Dove, Laughing 28**
☐☐ **Dove, Namaqua 31**
☐☐ Dove, Red Turtle
☐☐ **Dove, Rock 207**
☐☐ Dove, Rufous Turtle
☐☐ Dove, Stock
☐☐ Dowitcher, Long-billed
☐☐ Drongo, Black
☐☐ **Duck, Ferruginous 168**
☐☐ Duck, Fulvous Whistling
☐☐ Duck, Knob-billed
☐☐ Duck, Lesser Whistling
☐☐ Duck, Marbled
☐☐ **Duck, Tufted 169**
☐☐ **Dunlin 127**
☐☐ **Eagle, Bonelli's 199**
☐☐ **Eagle, Booted 247**
☐☐ **Eagle, Eastern Imperial 198**
☐☐ **Eagle, Golden 217**
☐☐ **Eagle, Greater Spotted 197**
☐☐ Eagle, Lesser Spotted
☐☐ Eagle, Pallas's Fish
☐☐ **Eagle, Short-toed Snake 200**
☐☐ **Eagle, Steppe 196**
☐☐ Eagle, Tawny
☐☐ **Eagle, Verreaux's 241**
☐☐ **Egret, Cattle 90**
☐☐ Egret, Intermediate
☐☐ **Egret, Little 148**
☐☐ **Egret, Western Great 149**
☐☐ Falcon, Amur
☐☐ Falcon, Barbary
☐☐ Falcon, Lanner
☐☐ Falcon, Peregrine
☐☐ Falcon, Saker
☐☐ **Falcon, Sooty 115**
☐☐ **Finch, Trumpeter 247**
☐☐ **Flamingo, Greater 157**
☐☐ Flamingo, Lesser
☐☐ **Flycatcher, African Paradise 231**
☐☐ Flycatcher, Asian Brown
☐☐ Flycatcher, Blue-and-white
☐☐ Flycatcher, Eurasian Pied
☐☐ Flycatcher, Red-breasted

☐☐ Flycatcher, Semi-collared
☐☐ **Flycatcher, Spotted 60**
☐☐ **Francolin, Grey 36**
☐☐ Frigatebird, Great
☐☐ Frigatebird, Lesser
☐☐ **Gadwall 165**
☐☐ Gallinule, Allen's
☐☐ Gannet, Cape
☐☐ **Garganey 161**
☐☐ **Godwit, Bar-tailed 131**
☐☐ **Godwit, Black-tailed 189**
☐☐ Goldfinch, European
☐☐ **Goose, Cotton Pygmy 242**
☐☐ Goose, Egyptian
☐☐ Goose, Greater White-fronted
☐☐ Goose, Greylag
☐☐ Goose, Lesser White-fronted
☐☐ Goshawk, Northern
☐☐ **Grebe, Black-necked 159**
☐☐ Grebe, Great Crested
☐☐ **Grebe, Little 158**
☐☐ **Greenshank, Common 184**
☐☐ Grosbeak, Arabian Golden-winged
☐☐ Gull, Baltic
☐☐ **Gull, Black-headed 102**
☐☐ Gull, Brown-headed
☐☐ **Gull, Caspian 101**
☐☐ Gull, Common
☐☐ **Gull, Great Black-headed 103**
☐☐ **Gull, Heuglin's 100**
☐☐ **Gull, Slender-billed 99**
☐☐ **Gull, Sooty 98**
☐☐ Gull, White-eyed
☐☐ Harrier, Hen
☐☐ **Harrier, Montagu's 93**
☐☐ **Harrier, Pallid 92**
☐☐ **Harrier, Western Marsh 171**
☐☐ Hawk-Cuckoo, Common
☐☐ Heron, Black
☐☐ **Heron, Black-crowned Night 150**
☐☐ Heron, Black-headed
☐☐ Heron, Goliath
☐☐ **Heron, Grey 146**

☐☐ **Heron, Indian Pond 153**
☐☐ **Heron, Purple 151**
☐☐ **Heron, Squacco 152**
☐☐ **Heron, Striated 116**
☐☐ **Heron, Western Reef 147**
☐☐ **Hobby, Eurasian 247**
☐☐ **Hoopoe, Eurasian 35**
☐☐ **Hoopoe-Lark, Greater 213**
☐☐ Hypocolius
☐☐ Ibis, African Sacred
☐☐ **Ibis, Glossy 154**
☐☐ **Jacana, Pheasant-tailed 243**
☐☐ **Kestrel, Common 95**
☐☐ **Kestrel, Lesser 94**
☐☐ **Kingfisher, Collared 142**
☐☐ **Kingfisher, Common 143**
☐☐ **Kingfisher, Grey-headed 239**
☐☐ Kingfisher, Malachite
☐☐ Kingfisher, Pied
☐☐ **Kite, Black 240**
☐☐ **Kite, Black-eared 240**
☐☐ Kite, Black-winged
☐☐ **Kite, Yellow-billed 240**
☐☐ Kittiwake, Black-legged
☐☐ **Knot, Great 247**
☐☐ Knot, Red
☐☐ Koel, Asian
☐☐ Lapwing, Northern
☐☐ **Lapwing, Red-wattled 84**
☐☐ Lapwing, Sociable
☐☐ Lapwing, Spur-winged
☐☐ **Lapwing, White-tailed 85**
☐☐ Lark, Bar-tailed
☐☐ **Lark, Bimaculated 41**
☐☐ **Lark, Crested 38**
☐☐ **Lark, Desert 212**
☐☐ Lark, Dunn's
☐☐ **Lark, Greater Short-toed 40**
☐☐ Lark, Lesser Short-toed
☐☐ Lark, Red-capped
☐☐ **Lark, Singing Bush 236**
☐☐ Lark, Thick-billed
☐☐ Magpie, Eurasian
☐☐ **Mallard 164**
☐☐ Martin, Brown-throated
☐☐ **Martin, Common House 45**
☐☐ Martin, Eurasian Crag
☐☐ Martin, Pale
☐☐ **Martin, Pale Crag 43**
☐☐ **Martin, Sand 44**
☐☐ Merganser, Red-breasted
☐☐ Merlin
☐☐ **Moorhen, Common 172**
☐☐ Moorhen, Lesser
☐☐ Munia, Scaly-breasted
☐☐ Myna, Bank
☐☐ **Myna, Common 26**
☐☐ **Nightingale, Common 246**
☐☐ Nightingale, Thrush
☐☐ Nightjar, Egyptian
☐☐ **Nightjar, European 81**
☐☐ Nightjar, Nubian
☐☐ Noddy, Brown
☐☐ Noddy, Lesser
☐☐ **Oriole, Eurasian Golden 83**
☐☐ **Osprey 114**
☐☐ Ouzel, Ring
☐☐ Owl, Arabian Scops
☐☐ **Owl, Barn 247**
☐☐ **Owl, Eurasian Scops 247**
☐☐ Owl, Hume's
☐☐ **Owl, Little 201**
☐☐ Owl, Long-eared
☐☐ Owl, Pallid Scops
☐☐ Owl, Pharaoh Eagle
☐☐ Owl, Short-eared
☐☐ Owl, Spotted Eagle
☐☐ **Oystercatcher, Eurasian 117**
☐☐ **Parakeet, Rose-ringed 27**
☐☐ **Partridge, Arabian 209**
☐☐ **Partridge, Chukar 208**
☐☐ **Partridge, Sand 210**
☐☐ Pelican, Dalmatian
☐☐ Pelican, Great White
☐☐ Pelican, Pink-backed
☐☐ Petrel, Jouanin's
☐☐ Phalarope, Grey
☐☐ **Phalarope, Red-necked 133**
☐☐ Phalarope, Wilson's
☐☐ **Pigeon, Bruce's Green 230**

☐☐ Pintail, **Northern 162**
☐☐ Pipit, Blyth's
☐☐ Pipit, Buff-bellied
☐☐ Pipit, Golden
☐☐ **Pipit, Long-billed 246**
☐☐ Pipit, Meadow
☐☐ Pipit, Olive-backed
☐☐ **Pipit, Red-throated 54**
☐☐ **Pipit, Richard's 246**
☐☐ **Pipit, Tawny 52**
☐☐ **Pipit, Tree 55**
☐☐ **Pipit, Water 53**
☐☐ Plover, American Golden
☐☐ Plover, Caspian
☐☐ **Plover, Common Ringed 120**
☐☐ Plover, Eurasian Golden
☐☐ **Plover, Greater Sand 123**
☐☐ **Plover, Grey 124**
☐☐ **Plover, Kentish 121**
☐☐ **Plover, Lesser Sand 122**
☐☐ **Plover, Little Ringed 87**
☐☐ **Plover, Pacific Golden 86**
☐☐ **Pochard, Common 167**
☐☐ Pochard, Red-crested
☐☐ Pratincole, Black-winged
☐☐ **Pratincole, Collared 88**
☐☐ **Pratincole, Small 247**
☐☐ **Prinia, Graceful 20**
☐☐ **Quail, Common 37**
☐☐ Quail, Harlequin
☐☐ Rail, Water
☐☐ **Raven, Brown-necked 215**
☐☐ **Raven, Fan-tailed 234**
☐☐ **Redshank, Common 182**
☐☐ **Redshank, Spotted 183**
☐☐ **Redstart, Black 56**
☐☐ **Redstart, Common 57**
☐☐ Redstart, Evermann's
☐☐ Robin, Black Scrub
☐☐ Robin, European
☐☐ **Robin, Rufous-tailed Scrub 68**
☐☐ Robin, White-throated
☐☐ **Rockfinch, Pale 247**
☐☐ **Roller, European 22**

☐☐ **Roller, Indian 23**
☐☐ Roller, Lilac-breasted
☐☐ Rosefinch, Common
☐☐ **Ruff 89**
☐☐ **Sanderling 128**
☐☐ **Sandgrouse, Chestnut-bell 67**
☐☐ **Sandgrouse, Crowned 220**
☐☐ **Sandgrouse, Lichtenstein's 222**
☐☐ Sandgrouse, Pin-tailed
☐☐ **Sandgrouse, Spotted 221**
☐☐ Sandpiper, Baird's
☐☐ **Sandpiper, Broad-billed 129**
☐☐ Sandpiper, Buff-breasted
☐☐ **Sandpiper, Common 188**
☐☐ **Sandpiper, Curlew 126**
☐☐ **Sandpiper, Green 187**
☐☐ **Sandpiper, Marsh 185**
☐☐ Sandpiper, Pectoral
☐☐ Sandpiper, Sharp-tailed
☐☐ **Sandpiper, Terek 130**
☐☐ **Sandpiper, Wood 186**
☐☐ **Serin, Yemen 237**
☐☐ Shearwater, Flesh-footed
☐☐ **Shearwater, Persian 138**
☐☐ Shearwater, Scopoli's
☐☐ Shearwater, Sooty
☐☐ Shearwater, Streaked
☐☐ Shearwater, Wedge-tailed
☐☐ **Shelduck, Common 170**
☐☐ Shelduck, Ruddy
☐☐ Shikra
☐☐ **Shoveler, Northern 163**
☐☐ Shrike, Bay-backed
☐☐ **Shrike, Isabelline 61**
☐☐ Shrike, Lesser Grey
☐☐ Shrike, Long-tailed
☐☐ **Shrike, Masked 65**
☐☐ **Shrike, Red-backed 247**
☐☐ **Shrike, Southern Grey 62**
☐☐ **Shrike, Steppe Grey 63**
☐☐ **Shrike, Turkestan 61**
☐☐ **Shrike, Woodchat 64**
☐☐ **Silverbill, African 227**
☐☐ **Silverbill, Indian 25**